Diplomica Verlag

Kathrin Schmidt
Katja Simone Wülfert

Practical Handbook for the Marketing of Foreign Investment Funds in Germany

A legal overview

Schmidt, Kathrin/Wülfert, Katja Simone: Practical Handbook for the Marketing
of Foreign Investment Funds in Germany, Hamburg, Diplomica Verlag GmbH

Umschlaggestaltung: Diplomica Verlag GmbH, Hamburg

ISBN: 978-3-8366-8626-6

© Diplomica Verlag GmbH, Hamburg 2010

Bibliografische Information der Deutschen Nationalbibliothek:

Die Deutsche Nationalbibliothek verzeichnet diese Publikation
in der Deutschen Nationalbibliografie;
detaillierte bibliografische Daten sind im Internet über
http://dnb.d-nb.de abrufbar.

Die digitale Ausgabe (eBook-Ausgabe) dieses Titels trägt die
ISBN 978-3-8366-3626-1 und kann über den Handel oder
den Verlag bezogen werden.

Disclaimer

This book provides legal information to non-German Investment Companies which intend to sell units of their investment funds in the German market. Legal information is, however, not the same as legal advice - the application of law to specific cases. This book is for general information only and not intended to provide legal advice for specific cases. The authors recommend that readers consult a lawyer or other professional adviser if professional assurance is needed that the information contained in this book, and any interpretation of it is appropriate in any specific case.

INDEX

LIST OF DEFINITIONS AND INTERNET LINKS

Az.	Reference number (*Aktenzeichen*)
BaFin	Federal Financial Supervisory Authority (*Bundesanstalt für Finanzdienstleistungsaufsicht*)
	http://www.bafin.de/
BaFin FAQs	Questionnaire relating to the notification of foreign UCITS in Germany dated 24.08.2009. (*Fragenkatalog zur Vertriebsanzeige nach §132 des Investmentgesetzes sowie zum Vertrieb ausländischer EG-Investmentanteile ("FAQ Ausländische UCITS"*))
	http://www.bafin.de/cln_179/SharedDocs/Downloads /DE/Service/Aufsichtsrecht/ucits__faq,templateId= raw,property=publicationFile.pdf/ucits_faq.pdf
BaFin Guidelines	BaFin Guidline (2008) for Notifications of EU-Investment Units for Public Distribution in the Federal Republic of Germany pursuant to §132 of the Investment Act as updated on 18.03.2008 (*Merkblatt (2008) für Anzeigen von EG-Investmentanteilen zum öffentlichen Vertrieb in der Bundesrepublik Deutschland nach §132 des Investmentgesetzes*)
	http://www.bafin.de/cln_179/SharedDocs/Downloads /DE/Service/Merkblaetter/mb__080107__anzeige invest,templateId=raw,property=publicationFile.pdf /mb_080107_anzeigeinvest.pdf
BaFin Marketing Guidelines	BaFin Circular letter 01/2010 (WA) 11 February 2010 (*Rundschreiben zur Auslegung der Vorschriften des Wertpapierhandelsgesetzes über Informationen einschließlich Werbung von Wertpapierdienstleistungsunternehmen an Kunden*),
	http://www.bafin.de/cln_152/nn_722758/SharedDocs /Veroeffentlichungen/DE/Service/Rundschreiben/ 2010/rs__1001__wa__Werbung.html
BGB	German Civil Code (*Bürgerliches Gesetzbuch*)
	http://dejure.org/gesetze/BGB

BGH	German High Court (*Bundesgerichtshof*)
BörsG	German Stock Exchange Act (*Börsengesetz*) http://dejure.org/gesetze/BoersG
B2B	business-to-business
B2C	business-to-consumer
CESR	Committee of European Securities Regulators http://www.cesr-eu.org
CESR Guidelines	CESR Guidelines to simplify the notification procedure of UCITS (Ref: CESR/06-120b), June 2006 http://www.cesr-eu.org/data/document/06_120b.pdf
Commission	Commission of the European Communities
CSSF	Luxembourg Commission de Surveillance du Secteur Financier
C2C	consumer-to-consumer
EEA	European Economic Area
EGBGB	Introductory Act to the Civil Code (*Einführungsgesetz zum Bürgerlichen Gesetzbuch*) http://www.gesetze-im-internet.de/ bgbeg/index.html
Elektronischer Bundesanzeiger	Electronic Federal Gazette (*elektronischer Bundesanzeiger*) http://www.ebundesanzeiger.de
ETF	Exchange Traded Fund
ETF & ETC Segment	The Exchange Traded Funds & Exchange Traded Commodities Segment of the FSE's Regulated Market
EU	European Union (*Europäische Union*)
EUR	The euro (sign: €; code: EUR) is the official currency of the European Union (EU)
FSE	Frankfurt Stock Exchange (*Frankfurter Wertpapierbörse*)

GewO	Code of Trade and Commerce (*Gewerbeordnung*)
	http://www.gesetze-im-internet.de/gewo
HGB	German Commercial Code (*Handelsgesetzbuch)*
	http://www.gesetze-im-internet.de/hgb
Host Member State	Member State other than the UCITS Home Member State in which its units are marketed
Host Member State Authority	authorities which the Host Member State has designated under Article 49 of the UCITS Directive
Home Member State	for UCITS and their Management Company the Member State in which the Management Company's registered office is situated
Home Member State Authority	authorities which the Home Member State has designated under Article 49 of the UCITS Directive
InvG	German Investment Act (*Investmentgesetz*)
	http://www.bafin.de/cln_171/nn_721188/SharedDocs /Aufsichtsrecht/DE/Gesetze/invg__ab__100611.html ?__nnn=true
InvStG	German Investment Tax Act (*Investmentsteuergesetz*)
	http://www.gesetze-im-internet.de/invstg /BJNR272400003.html
Investment Company	for investment funds set up in contractual form (such as a Luxembourg *Fonds commun de placement*) or trust form (unit trust/common fund), the company whose regular business is collective portfolio management of the fund
	for investment funds set up in corporate form (such as a Luxembourg Sicav or an Irish plc), the company itself
Issuer Guidelines	guidelines for issuers issued by the BaFin on 28 April 2009 (*Emittentenleitfaden*)
	http://www.bafin.de/cln_161/nn_721290/SharedDocs /Downloads/DE/Service/Leitfaeden/emittentenleitfad en__2009,templateId=raw,property=publicationFile. pdf/emittentenleitfaden_2009.pdf

KWG	German Banking Act (*Kreditwesengesetz*)
	http://www.bafin.de/cln_179/nn_721188/SharedDocs /Aufsichtsrecht/DE/Gesetze/kwg__ab__100611.html ?__nnn=true
Management Board	Management Board (executive body) of the FSE
Management Company	for UCITS set up in contractual form (such as a Luxembourg Fcp) or trust form (unit trust/common fund), the company whose regular business is the collective portfolio management of the UCITS
	for UCITS set up in corporate form (such as a Luxembourg Sicav or an Irish plc), the company itself
Member State	an EEA state
MiFID	Directive 2004/39/EC of the European Parliament and of the Council of 21 April 2004 on markets in financial instruments amending Council Directives 85/611/EEC and 93/6/EEC and Directive 2000/12/EC of the European Parliament and of the Council and repealing Council Directive 93/22/EEC
	http://eur-lex.europa.eu/LexUriServ/LexUriServ.do? uri=CELEX:32004L0039:EN:HTML
NAV	net asset value (*Nettoinventarwert*)
no.	number
Non-UCITS	foreign investment asset pools which have not obtained a UCITS passport or which originate from a country outside the EEA
Organised Market	a multilateral system operated and/or managed by a market operator which brings together or facilitates the bringing together of multiple third-party buying and selling interests in financial instruments, in the system and in accordance with its non-discretionary rules, in a way which results in a contract, in respect of the financial instruments admitted to trading under its rules and/or systems, and which is authorised and functions regularly and in accordance with the

provisions of Title III of the MiFID (Article 4.1(14), MiFID*)*

The annotated presentation of regulated markets and national provisions implementing relevant requirements of MiFID provides an official list of the Organised Markets in the EU and EEA

http://eur-lex.europa.eu/LexUriServ/LexUriServ.do?uri=OJ:C:2009:158:0003:0008:EN:PDF

p.	page
Regulated Market	the German Organised Market within the meaning of §32 BörsG
Regulated Unofficial Market	a German non-official and unregulated market segment within the meaning of §48 BörsG. At the FSE the Regulated Unofficial Market is also called the Open Market (*Freiverkehr*)
UCITS	Undertakings for Collective Investment in Transferable Securities which comply with the UCITS Directive
UCITS Directive or UCITS III	Council Directive of 20 December 1985 on the co-ordination of laws, regulations and administrative provisions relating to undertakings for collective investment in transferable securities (Official Journal EC no. L 375 page 3) Directive 85/611/EEC, as amended by Directive 2008/18/EC of the European Parliament and of the Council (OJ L 76, 19.3.2008, p. 42)

http://eur-lex.europa.eu/LexUriServ/LexUriServ.do?uri=CONSLEG:1985L0611:20080320:EN:PDF

UCITS IV Directive or UCITS IV	Directive 2009/65/EC of the European Parliament and of the Council of 13 July 2009 on the coordination of laws, regulations and administrative provisions relating to undertakings for collective investment in transferable securities (UCITS) (recast)

	http://eur-lex.europa.eu/LexUriServ/LexUriServ.do? uri=OJ:L:2009:302:0032:0096:EN:PDF
	It is expected that the Commission will adopt implementing measures clarifying certain elements of the Directive by July 2010. Member States will be required to transpose the provisions of the Directive and the implementing measures into national law and implement them by 1 July 2011.
UWG	Act on Unfair Competition (*Gesetz gegen unlauteren Wettbewerb*)
	http://www.gesetze-im-internet.de/uwg_2004
VerkprospektG	Sales Prospectus Act (*Verkaufsprospektgesetz)*
	http://www.gesetze-im-internet.de/verkaufsprospektg /BJNR127490990.html
VwVfG	Administrative Procedures Act (*Verwaltungsverfahrensgesetz*)
	http://www.gesetze-im-internet.de/vwvfg/index.html
WpHG	German Securities Trading Act (*Wertpapierhandelsgesetz*)
	http://dejure.org/gesetze/WpHG
WpPG	German Securities Prospectus Act (*Wertpapierprospektgesetz*)
	http://dejure.org/gesetze/WpPG
WpDVerOV	Regulation on the Specification of the Rules of Conduct and the Organisational Requirements for Investment Services Enterprises (*Verordnung zur Konkretisierung der Verhaltensregeln und Organisationsanforderungen für Wertpapierdienstleistungsun-ternehmen, Wertpapierdienstleistungs-Verhaltens- und Organisationsverordnung, WpDVerOV*)
	http://www.gesetze-im-internet.de/wpdverov /index.html

WM Daten

WM Data Service (*WM Datenservice, Herausgebergemeinschaft der Wertpapier-Mitteilungen*)

http://www.wmdaten.de

CHAPTER 1 - PREFACE

German law differentiates between regulated and unregulated funds. This book deals with regulated foreign investment funds under the Investment Act. The Investment Act governs the public distribution of EU-harmonised UCITS funds and non-UCITS funds meeting certain formal requirements. A substantial portion of funds is not covered by it, in particular foreign closed-end non-regulated funds. The regulatory framework applicable to such funds is outlined in chapter 2.2.

This book can be used as a manual for:

- notification with the BaFin of UCITS for public distribution in Germany;

- German law issues in relation to fund marketing and distribution of regulated funds;

- private placements of regulated funds when public distribution is not intended;

- listing regulated funds on a German stock exchange and

- questions of compliance following a BaFin notification or a stock exchange listing.

This book provides legal information to non-German Investment Companies which intend to sell the units of their investment funds in the German market.

The cut-off date for legal developments included in this book is 31 March 2010. The Investment Act, the Banking Act and the Civil Code are taken into account in their versions of 11 June 2010.

CHAPTER 2 - CATEGORISATION OF FOREIGN FUNDS

2.1 Investment funds under the Investment Act

The Investment Act applies to foreign investment units in foreign investment asset pools. For foreign investment units to come within the scope of the Investment Act, they must be issued by an enterprise whose registered seat is abroad, i.e. a foreign Investment Company, and must provide their unitholders with a redemption right or, if they do not, the foreign Investment Company must be subject to investment supervision (§2 para (9) InvG).

2.1.1 UCITS

2.1.1.1 Definition

The criteria mentioned in chapter 2.1 are always fulfilled with regard to UCITS.

The units of a UCITS are defined in §2 para (10) InvG as foreign investment units in an investment asset pool which is subject to the law of another Member State of the EU or another contracting state to the agreement on the EEA, and which have been issued by an Investment Company whose seat is in such a state, and which comply with the requirements of the UCITS Directive.

For the purposes of the UCITS Directive, UCITS are undertakings:

- whose sole object is collective investment;

- comprising capital raised from the public;

- in transferable securities and/or in other liquid financial assets as defined in the Directive;

- which spread risk; and

- whose units, at holders' request, are repurchased or redeemed, directly or indirectly, out of the assets of the undertaking.

UCITS may be constituted under the law of contract as common funds managed by management companies, under trust law as unit trusts or under company law as investment companies.

2.1.1.2 Passport procedure

UCITS can be marketed freely within the EEA, subject to a notification or passport procedure (see chapters 2.1.1.2 and 4.1). Collective investment schemes which comply with the UCITS Directive as implemented into the national law of their Home Member State are authorised as UCITS by their Home Member State Authority. This authorisation allows such UCITS to market publicly their units in their Home Member State as well as in all other Member States. To market its units in another Member State, the UCITS only needs to be notified to the respective Host Member State Authority, which in Germany is the BaFin, in accordance with Article 46 of the UCITS Directive as implemented into the national law of the Host Member State.

Pursuant to the UCITS Directive's principle of home country control (Article 49 para (3) sentence 1 UCITS Directive), the Host Member State Authority does not have authority to review the fund's compliance with the Directive. The Home Member State is solely responsible for fund authorisation, fund structure, fund management, investment policies and scope, contents and timing of information which must be supplied to unitholders. In respect of matters reserved for the Home Members State, the Host Member State has no powers to impose additional rules, requirements or information requests.

However, a UCITS which markets its units in another Member State must comply with the laws, regulations and administrative provisions in force in that state which do not fall within the competence of the UCITS Directive (Article 49 para (3) sentence 2 UCITS Directive). Article 44 (1) of the UCITS-Directive states: "*A UCITS which markets its units in another Member State must comply with the laws, regulations and administrative provisions in force in that State which do not fall within the field governed by this Directive*". The Host Member State retains responsibility for distribution infrastructure, techniques and channels, advertising, facilities for making payments to unitholders, repurchase or redemption of units and for making information on the UCITS available to the unitholders (Articles 44 and 45 of the UCITS Directive).

As a result, before a UCITS is admitted for public marketing in Germany and during the course of the notification, the BaFin formally inspects the fund documentation. It checks that the information which must be provided to investors relating to facilities for making payments, repurchase or redemption as prescribed by the Investment Act (see chapter

4.3.2.3.2) has been properly included and that planned marketing and distribution channels or methods do not contravene German law. In satisfying itself as to these matters, the BaFin can request further information (see chapters 4.1.3 and 4.1.4). If the BaFin is of the view that German law would be breached, it may prohibit public marketing of the UCITS (see chapter 4.1.5).

Since the UCITS Directive was implemented into German law in 1990, the number of passport notifications submitted to the BaFin has steadily increased year on year. In 2008[1], the BaFin processed 1,540 notifications of funds or sub-funds for public distribution in Germany. Most UCITS in 2008 originated from Luxembourg and Ireland, followed by Austria and France. In 2008, a total of 8,266 UCITS (after mergers and liquidations) were notified for public distribution in Germany[2].

2.1.1.3 UCITS IV Directive

The BaFin's regulatory powers as Host Member State Authority will be curtailed once the UCITS IV Directive comes into effect. One of the most important aspects of UCITS IV is that it will replace the current notification procedure by a regulator to regulator procedure, with the object of compelling national regulators to remove administrative barriers between one another and generally to improve their working practices in order to facilitate quicker EEA market access for UCITS.

Under the UCITS Directive, the Host Member State Authority is not permitted to review, challenge or discuss the merits of the UCITS authorisation granted by the Home Member State Authority. UCITS IV will in addition bar the Host Member State Authority from checking compliance with applicable Host Member State national law which is outside the scope of the Directive *before* the UCITS commences marketing in the Host Member State. The BaFin will continue to check and enforce compliance with applicable German law, but only *after* the UCITS has commenced marketing its units in Germany.

Under UCITS IV, the BaFin will still be authorised to check that marketing by the Management Company complies with national law, subject to such control by the BaFin not being discriminatory and not preventing the UCITS from accessing the German

---

[1] Being the last year for which data is available.
[2] *Jahresbericht der Bundesanstalt für Finanzdienstleistungsaufsicht 2008*, chapter VI: *Aufsicht über den Wertpapierhandel und das Investmentgeschäft*, p. 51.
http://www.bafin.de/nn_992916/SharedDocs/Downloads/DE/Service/Jahresberichte/2008/ jb_2008_kapitel_VI.html

market. The BaFin's powers do not extend to checking key investor information, the prospectus or annual and semi-annual reports.

The UCITS IV Directive provides that Member State authorities must ensure that Management Companies which market UCITS cross-border have easy access via electronic publication to full information on the applicable laws, regulations and administrative requirements in the Host Member State. Member States must make such information available in a language customary in international finance, in a clear and unambiguous manner. This information should be kept up-to-date. CESR's guidance is that such information cannot be relied on as exhaustive and must be without prejudice to other provisions of the Host Member State's national law.[3]

2.1.1.4 Private placements and stock exchange listings

UCITS can be privately placed in Germany subject to rigorous private placement rules (see chapter 3) and may be listed on a German stock exchange (see chapter 8). A prerequisite for investment funds to apply for listing on the Deutsche Börse's ETF segment, however, is the prior BaFin notification for public distribution in Germany (see chapter 8.2.3.2.2).

2.1.2 Non-UCITS

2.1.2.1 Definition

Foreign investment asset pools which have not obtained a UCITS passport or which originate from a country outside the EEA will come within the scope of the Investment Act, provided that:

1. they grant unitholders the right to redeem their units or are subject to investment supervision (§2 para (9) InvG); and
2. they qualify as asset pools for collective investment of capital and are invested in accordance with the principle of risk diversification in assets within the meaning of §2 para (4) InvG (§1 sentence 2 InvG and §2 para (8) InvG).

---

[3]   "CESR's technical advice to the European Commission on level 2 measures relating to mergers of UCITS, master-feeder UCITS structures and crossborder notification of UCITS", December 2009, Ref.: CESR/09-1186, no. 3.1, explanatory text 9.
http://www.cesr.eu/data/document/09_1186_Final_advice_Part_III_UCITS_IV_for_publication.pdf

On 22 December 2008, the BaFin in coordination with the German Ministry of Finance issued circular 14/2008[4] to explain its administrative practice concerning the applicability of the Investment Act to foreign investment schemes. A further explanatory note was issued on 21 January 2010[5]. A foreign Investment Company which intends to offer units either publicly or by private placement in Germany should use the circular and note to determine if the fund falls within the scope of the Investment Act, failing which other regulatory regimes may need to be considered, in particular the Securities Prospectus Act (*Wertpapierhandelsgesetz, WpPG*) or Sales Prospectus Act (*Verkaufsprospektgesetz, VerkprospektG*).

Prospectus requirements for public distribution of fund products which fall outside the scope of the Investment Act but qualify as securities, are governed by the German Securities Prospectus Act which implements the European Prospectus Directive (2003/71/EC)[6] into German law. The issuer has to meet the disclosure requirement of EU prospectus law (EU-Regulation 809/2004)[7] unless it comes within an exemption under the Prospectus Directive. Public distribution of financial products which neither qualify as investment funds nor as securities is likely to be subject to the prospectus requirements of German Sales Prospectus Act.

The circular and the note provide that the BaFin no longer issues advance rulings on the applicability of the Investment Act to non-UCITS, but instead it makes a determination only on a fund's complete registration filing for public marketing in Germany. The BaFin bases its determination on the fund rules or the articles of incorporation of the Investment Company, as well as on the prospectus and any written statements to the BaFin by the applicant.

---

[4] "*Rundschreiben 14/2008 (WA) zum Anwendungsbereich des Investmentgesetzes nach §1 Satz 1 Nr. 3 InvG*", 22.12.2008.
http://www.bafin.de/cln_109/nn_722754/SharedDocs/Veroeffentlichungen/DE/Service/Rundschreiben/2008/rs__1408__wa.html

[5] "*Fragenkatalog zum Anwendungsbereich des Investmentgesetzes nach §1 Satz 1 Nr. 3 InvG und zum Rundschreiben 14/2008 (WA)*", 19.05.2009.
http://www.bafin.de/nn_722754/SharedDocs/Veroeffentlichungen/DE/Service/Auslegungsentscheidungen/Wertpapieraufsicht/ae__100121__invg.html

[6] http://eur-lex.europa.eu/LexUriServ/LexUriServ.do?uri=OJ:L:2003:345:0064:0089:EN:PDF

[7] http://ec.europa.eu/internal_market/securities/docs/prospectus/reg-2004-809/reg-2004-809_en.pdf

2.1.2.1.1 Right to redeem units

The majority of unitholders must have a periodic right to redeem their units. Agreements between the Investment Company and a minority of shareholders will be discounted in the assessment of whether such a right to redeem exists. Redemption prices can be paid in cash or kind. Arrangements to ensure that the quotation of the units does not deviate materially from their NAV are also regarded as redemptions, such as the redemption of creation units in case of ETFs (see chapter 8.1 for ETF redemption units).

In the case of umbrella funds, the BaFin treats each sub-fund separately but does not treat unit classes separately.

The right to redeem units at predetermined dates is sufficient to qualify, provided that investors have a redemption right at least once during a two year period. If redemption is permitted less often than that, the fund will be considered closed-end. The fund will also be categorised as closed-end if the Investment Company has a discretion to decline a unitholder's request to exercise its redemption right.

Lock-up periods which suspend the unitholders' right of redemption for a specified time after purchase are permitted, provided that after the lock-up period has expired, investors are permitted to redeem their units at least once during a two year period. The lock-up period may last longer than two years. The BaFin applies the same principle to redemption deadlines where payment for the units to be redeemed is made at a specified time, which is later either than when the unitholder exercises its right to redeem or when the units are returned to the Investment Company.

The BaFin will regard an obligation of a third party other than the Investment Company to buy units, as a redemption right within the meaning of the Investment Act, provided that the units have to be purchased at their NAV and funds are available to complete the purchase. This is only the case if the Investment Company's constitutive documents (fund rules of the investment fund or the articles of association of the investment fund company) state that it would be liquidated if it is not able to provide such third party with the necessary financial resources to fulfil its repurchase obligations.

A right of redemption within the meaning of the Investment Act requires that an investor redeeming its units can claim payment of the full amount of its portion of the NAV of the fund. The redemption price can be net of redemption charges, transaction fees and similar deductions as long as these deductions do not result in reductions of the NAV by more than

15%. The fund documentation may contain a cap on the value of the right to redeem, provided that the cap protects unitholders' interests.

2.1.2.1.2. Foreign investment fund supervision

In the case of closed-end foreign investment funds which do not give investors a redemption right as described in chapter 2.1.2.1.1, the BaFin looks at the nature and extent of supervision in the fund's home country to decide if the level of supervision is sufficient for the fund to come within the scope of the Investment Act. The result can vary for different funds even in relation to the same foreign supervisor. If it is not convinced as a result of its own enquiries, the BaFin may require proof from the Investment Company that satisfactory investment supervision exists.

The BaFin requires the Investment Company to be supervised by a public body. Such supervision must encompass investor protection. The BaFin will deem the supervision to be satisfactory if, for example, the competent foreign regulator is satisfied that:

1. prior to issuing units in the fund, the Investment Company is solvent;

2. its management is reliable and qualified; and

3. after units have been issued, the portfolio structure complies with legal and statutory requirements, including investment limits.

The BaFin has stated that it considers these requirements fulfilled in respect of the CSSFs supervision of Luxembourg SICARs (*Société d'investissement en capital à risque* – undertaking for collective venture capital investment). However, since SICARs are not subject to minimum diversification rules, they might not fulfil the risk diversification requirement as set out in chapter 2.1.2.1.4.

The following measures do not qualify as investment fund supervision:

1. supervision which is targeted at the integrity and capability of the market;

2. supervision relating to certain tax requirements; or

3. an obligation merely to register a fund in its home country.

2.1.2.1.3 Asset pool for collective investment of capital

Asset pools for collective investment of capital are independent entities. Their objective business purpose is primarily the investment and administration of assets for the collective account of investors.

"Collective" requires that the investment is open to more than one investor, even if the fund in practice only has one investor. The legal structure of the asset pool and the legal nature of its investors, whether they are natural or legal persons, are irrelevant. The investor's interest in the asset pool does not need to be a membership: it is sufficient if the investor has an economic stake in the opportunities and risks of the collective investment scheme.

As the BaFin explained in the draft circular of 9 June 2008[8], collective investments of capital should not be confused with individual portfolio management, where the investor's interest is in the assets themselves, rather than in the portfolio of assets as a whole.

2.1.2.1.4 Risk diversification

The portfolio's objective business purpose under its constitutive documents must be risk diversification.

Risk diversification means that the portfolio should comprise more than three assets, each of which has different investment risks. These risks can derive from the type of securities, the issuer's credit ratings, market risks, domestic, international or other regional circumstances, currency risks, income potential or maturities. Assets held in the portfolio must be for investment and not for liquidity or other purposes. It is not sufficient if risk diversification is incidental to the strategy for investing and administrating the portfolio. If the portfolio's investment purpose is not risk diversification, but it happens to comprise at least three assets with different investment risks, it will not qualify as an investment fund under the Investment Act.

Indirect risk diversification, for example through master feeder structures, will suffice. Risk diversification will be deemed to have been complied with if to a more than insignificant extent an investment asset pool contains units in one or more other portfolios,

---

[8] *"Konsultation 9/2008 – Entwurf des Rundschreibens zum Anwendungsbereich des Investmentgesetzes nach §1 Satz 1 Nr. 3 InvG"*, 09.06.2008.
http://www.bafin.de/nn_1522846/SharedDocs/Veroeffentlichungen/DE/Unternehmen/Konsultationen/2008/kon__0908__Anwendungsber__InvG.html

and such other portfolios are invested directly or indirectly in accordance with risk diversification principles (§2 para (8) sentence 2 InvG). Such other portfolios do not themselves need to qualify as investment asset pools under the Investment Act, provided that they qualify as real estate companies (as defined in §2 para (4) no. 6 InvG) or PPP project companies (as defined in §2 para (14) InvG).

If in breach of its constitutive documents an Investment Company fails to observe risk diversification principles, it will not be allowed to market its units publicly in Germany. If the breach occurs after the fund has been successfully registered for public distribution, the BaFin will prohibit further public distribution.

2.1.2.1.5 Eligible assets

For an asset pool to be regarded as a foreign investment fund under the Investment Act, it must have or pursuant to its objective business purpose aim to have, more than 90% of its NAV directly invested in assets within the meaning of §2 para (4) InvG.

Permitted investments pursuant to §2 para (4) InvG are:

1. securities;

2. money market instruments;

3. derivatives;

4. bank deposits;

5. real estate, rights equivalent to real estate and comparable rights under the laws of other states (real property);

6. interests in companies which, pursuant to their partnership agreement or articles of association, may only acquire real property and assets necessary to manage the real property (real property companies). This includes interests in companies which themselves acquire participations in real property companies;

7. units in certain other investment funds pursuant to §§50, 66, 83, 90g and 112 InvG and in corresponding foreign investment funds;

8. for infastructure funds within the meaning of §90a InvG and for comparable foreign funds, participations in PPP project companies, if the market value of such participations can be determined;

9. for domestic investment funds within the meaning of §90g InvG and comparable foreign investment funds ("cutting-edge funds") as additional assets: precious metals, unsecuritised loan obligations and equity participations, provided that their market value can be determined. Unsecuritised loan obligations only include loan obligations which have been acquired by the Investment Company through debt assignment and not through own-lending transactions. Equity participations within the meaning of no. 9 and 11 include shares in private equity funds (see chapters 2.2.1 and 2.2.4.2.1) and closed-end funds, provided that investors have property rights (for example profit-sharing rights) and administrative rights (for example voting or information rights) in the fund;

10. for domestic investment funds within the meaning of §112 InvG, for comparable foreign investment funds (single hedge funds, see chapter 2.1.2.2.2) and for investment stock corporations, silent participations within the meaning of §230 HGB in an enterprise which has its seat and management in Germany, provided that their market value can be determined; and

11. for domestic investment funds within the meaning of §112 InvG (single hedge funds) and for foreign investment funds whose investment policies are subject to requirements comparable to those in §112 para (1) InvG (see chapter 2.1.2.2), as additional assets: precious metals and equity participations, if their market value can be determined.

2.1.2.1.6 Investment limits

Investment limits to which the Investment Act subjects German investment funds are irrelevant for a foreign asset pool to qualify as an investment fund under the Investment Act, except for the following, which should feature in the Investment Company's constitutive documents, or in a side letter. In order to qualify as a foreign investment fund, mutual funds have to comply with the following investment restrictions:

1. not more than 20% of the fund's NAV in equity participations which are not admitted for trading in a stock exchange or included in an organised market within the meaning of §2 para (13) InvG, i.e. a market which is recognised and open to the public and which functions in an orderly manner (§90h para (4) sentence 1 InvG);

2. not more than 30% of the fund's NAV jointly in precious metals, unsecuritised loans and certain derivatives (§90h para (5) sentence 1 InvG); and

3. at least 60% of an infastructure fund's NAV in participations in PPP project companies, real estate and lifehold property interests (*Niessbrauch*) (§90b para (5) InvG).

Spezialfonds (special funds), comprising portfolios which are only offered to legal persons on the basis of a written contract with the Investment Company, but not to natural persons as investors, and single hedge funds, have to comply with the investment limits for equity participations which are not admitted to trading on a stock exchange or included in an organised market within the meaning of §2 para (13) InvG in order to qualify as investment funds under the Investment Act as follows:

1. up to 30% for hedge funds (§112 para (1) sentence 3 InvG); and

2. up to 20% for *Spezialfonds* (§91 para (3) no. 3 in connection with §90h para (4) sentence 1 InvG).

If a *Spezialfonds* or single hedge fund by its objective business purpose invests amongst others in equity participations, the above investment limits must be included in its constitutive documents.

2.1.2.1.7 Subject to the laws of another country

An asset pool is subject to the laws of a country other than Germany if the portfolio's legal structure, constitutive documents, investment limits or comparable provisions which determine the legal relationship between investors and the asset pool are governed by the laws of another country or one of its member states.

2.1.2.2 BaFin registration

Non-UCITS which are subject to the Investment Act may be publicly offered in Germany if registered with the BaFin (§135 et seq InvG and BaFin's preliminary guidelines for notifications pursuant to §139 InvG as amended and supplemented[9]). In 2008, a total of 115 non-UCITS funds were registered with the BaFin for public marketing in Germany. Nineteen new registrations were admitted, including fund of hedge funds and one open real estate fund. The BaFin statistics show that the number of non-UCITS registered for public marketing in Germany has been decreasing constantly from 2003 (328 funds) to 2008 (115 funds).[10]

2.1.2.2.1 General

The fund will be permitted to start public marketing three months after a complete registration filing with the BaFin has been made, unless the BaFin prohibits public marketing during this three months waiting period. The BaFin will confirm the date of receipt of the notification within four weeks of filing, and will require that missing information and documents are submitted by way of a supplementary notification. The supplementary notification must be submitted to the BaFin within six months of submission of the notification or, if applicable, the last supplementary notification. If the submission is not made within this timescale, the BaFin will prohibit public marketing. The three months waiting period only starts to run once the filing is complete.

During the three months waiting period, by checking and if necessary requesting changes to the fund documentation, the BaFin ensures that the level of protection for German investors in a non-UCITS fund is comparable to that for investors in German regulated investment funds (§§136 and 137 InvG), i.e. the fund assets must be held in custody or, if the fund assets comprise real estate, the portfolio must be supervised by a depository bank which exercises the prescribed level of control over the investment fund. The constitutive documents of the Investment Company must provide for certain protective requirements, including as to the transfer of fund units to investors, repayment of the portion of the fund

---

[9] *"Vorläufiges Merkblatt für Anzeigen nach §132 und §139 InvG sowie §144 Abs. 2 Satz 3 InvG in Verbindung mit § 15c AuslInvestmG"*, 30.12.2003.
http://www.bafin.de/cln_171/SharedDocs/Downloads/DE/Unternehmen/Fonds/Investmentfonds/031230 ,templateId=raw,property=publicationFile.pdf/031230.pdf
"Nachtrag 2 zum vorläufigen Merkblatt für Anzeigen nach §132 und §139 InvG sowie §144 Abs. 2 Satz 3 InvG in Verbindung mit §15c AuslInvestmG", 20.07.2004.
http://www.bafin.de/cln_171/SharedDocs/Downloads/DE/Unternehmen/Fonds/Investmentfonds/ 031230__nachtrag2,templateId=raw,property=publicationFile.pdf/031230_nachtrag2.pdf

[10] *Jahresbericht der Bundesanstalt für Finanzdienstleistungsaufsicht 2008*, see footnote 2, chapter VI, p. 52.

represented by its units, the acquisition of other funds by the fund and limitations on encumbrances, borrowings and short sales of fund assets. Special requirements apply to funds of hedge funds (§136 para (4) and §137 para (4) InvG).

The Investment Company must evidence to the BaFin that it is subject to effective public supervision in its home country. The BaFin needs to be satisfied that in its experience the competent supervisory authority is willing to cooperate with it.[11] The Investment Company must appoint a German credit institution or a reliable, suitably professionally qualified person as its German representative. It must also appoint at least one German credit institution or a German branch of a non-German credit institution as its German paying agent.

2.1.2.2.2 Single hedge funds

Single hedge funds (*Sondervermögen mit zusätzlichen Risiken,* funds with additional risks) are barred altogether from public marketing in Germany. Under §112 InvG, single hedge funds are investment asset pools which observe the principle of risk diversification and are not otherwise subject, according to their investment strategies, to limitations on asset selection pursuant to §2 para 4 nos. 1 to 4 and nos. 7, 10 and 11 InvG (see chapter 2.1.2.1.5.) The fund's constitutive documents must also provide for at least one of the following conditions (§112 para (1) InvG):

1. an increase in the fund's investment level through generally unlimited borrowings for the collective account of the investors or through using derivatives (leverage);

2. the sale of assets for the collective account of investors, which when the transaction is concluded, do not belong to the fund (short sale).

2.1.2.2.3 Funds of hedge funds

Funds of hedge funds (*Dach-Sondervermögen mit zusätzlichen Risiken,* funds of funds with additional risks) can be registered for public distribution with the BaFin if their

---

[11] Apart from funds originating from other EU countries, to date the BaFin has only admitted Swiss and U.S. funds. See the list of non-UCITS funds, which are permitted for public marketing in Germany and which is published and regularly updated by the BaFin:
"*Vertriebsberechtigte ausländische nicht EU-richtlinienkonforme Investmentfonds und vertriebsberechtigte ausländische Dach-Sondervermögen mit zusätzlichen Risiken*", 01.03.2010.
http://www.bafin.de/cln_161/nn_722552/SharedDocs/Downloads/DE/Verbraucher/Angebotsunterlagen/nonucits__pdf.html?__nnn=true

investment policy is comparable to that of German funds of hedge funds. Funds of hedge funds are defined in §113 InvG as investment asset pools which invest in units of target funds within the meaning of §112 InvG, in investment stock corporations pursuant to §96 InvG whose articles of association provide for an investment form comparable to §112 para (1) InvG, or in foreign investment asset pools which, with regard to their investment policy, are subject to requirements comparable to those in §112 para (1) InvG. They must invest at least 51% in single hedge funds and no more than 49% in liquidity. Foreign exchange financial instruments are only permitted for hedging currency risks. Leverage and short sales may not be effected by the Investment Company for funds of hedge funds (§136 para (4) in connection with §113 para (1) and (2) InvG).

2.1.2.3 Private placement and stock exchange listing

Another way of reaching the German public is through a stock exchange listing (see chapter 8). Non-UCITS can be listed on a stock exchange without being registered with the BaFin. This is because the trading of foreign investment units which are admitted to the Regulated Market or introduced to the Regulated Unofficial Market (*Freiverkehr*) of a German stock exchange is deemed to be a private placement, provided that only those announcements prescribed by the exchange are made in respect of the fund and no other public marketing of units takes place (see chapter 3.1.2.2.7). A prerequisite for investment funds to apply to be listed on the Deutsche Börse's ETF segment, however, is to have obtained prior BaFin registration for public distribution in Germany (see chapter 8.2.3.2.2).

Non-UCITS, including single hedge funds, can be privately placed in Germany, subject to restrictive private placement rules (see chapter 3).

2.2 Fund structures outside the Investment Act

Financial instruments may qualify as investment funds in their country of origin or may be called investment funds by their initiator, without being characterised as such under the Investment Act. In its circular 14/2008[12], the BaFin explained that private equity funds, certain debt instruments and certificates will not qualify as investment funds under the Investment Act.

---

[12] See footnote 4.

2.2.1 Private equity

Investment schemes of which more than 30% is targeted at equity participations with the intention of adding value through active management, fall outside the scope of the Investment Act.

The BaFin regards the following activities as indicators of active management operations:

1. projected or actual acquisition of the majority or a blocking minority of the shares in a company;

2. involvement in target companies other than by the exercise of shareholders' rights in sharcholders' meetings, such as acquiring decision-making powers and responsibility by appointment to relevant bodies at the target company, such as the supervisory board;

3. completing a thorough review of target company data which is not accessible to the general public, such as due diligence, prior to making the investment;

4. cooperating with third parties in a way which is likely substantially or permanently to affect the development of the target company; or

5. supporting active entrepreneurial activities of one or more other private equity funds.

These guidelines are focussed on private equity funds and do not apply to infrastructure funds, which are covered by the Investment Act.

2.2.2 Debt instruments

Debt instruments, such as consumer asset backed securities (consumer ABS), commercial mortgage backed securities (CMBS), collaterised bond obligations (CBO), collaterised loan obligations (CLO) or collaterised debt obligations (CDO), which are issued by a special purpose vehicle with its registered seat abroad in order to finance its portfolio, generally do not qualify as foreign investment units under the Investment Act. This is because their objective business purpose does not primarily lie in investment and administration of assets for the collective account of investors, but in other objectives such as increasing the originator's liquidity.

2.2.3 Certificates

Financial instruments such as bonus shares (*Genussscheine*) or participating certificates which link investor redemptions and/or dividends to the performance of a reference portfolio/investment fund or reference index of portfolios/ investment funds, typically do not qualify as investment fund units. This is mainly because the investor is not entitled to the assets which the certificates are based on or benchmarked against. The investor's claim is limited to performance of the instrument, and this in turn depends on how the underlying assets perform. The issuer of the certificates is not obliged to invest capital received from investors in eligible assets as described in chapter 2.1.2.1.5 other than for hedging purposes.

Certificates may qualify as investment fund units under the Investment Act if the issuer invests in eligible assets for the collective account of investors or if the investor enters into a direct relationship with the reference portfolio and, in each case, the investor has a direct interest in the portfolio. It is not a requirement that the investor's interest has the nature of a membership, but the portfolio must fulfil the requirements for a foreign investment fund as explained in chapter 2.1.

2.2.4 Collective investment management

2.2.4.1 Banking Act (*Kreditwesengesetz, KWG*)

Since 26 March 2009, German and foreign investment schemes which do not come within the scope of the Investment Act, in particular closed-end non-regulated funds, require a financial services licence irrespective of their legal personality or seat, if they render collective investment management services (*Anlageverwaltung*) in Germany (§1 para (1) a sentence 2, no. 11 KWG).

Investment schemes which qualify as foreign investment funds within the meaning of the Investment Act are not subject to the new licence requirements under the Banking Act (§2 para (6) no. 5b KWG). This exemption applies both to foreign investment funds which are offered to the German public, because the Investment Act as *lex specialis* prevails over the Banking Act, and also to private placements which are not covered by the Investment Act, because the German legislator did not intend that the new licence requirement should regulate the private placement of investment funds.[13]

§1 para (1) a sentence 2, no. 11 KWG defines "investment management" as:

- the purchase and sale of financial instruments;

- for a community of investors who are natural persons;

- with discretion in the selection of financial instruments;

- provided that this activity is a focus of the product offered; and

- is for the purpose of allowing these investors to participate in the performance of the acquired financial instruments.

The vehicle which purchases and sells financial instruments must obtain the licence, provided that it offers investment management services in Germany. This is the case if it has its registered seat, a branch office or another physical presence in Germany, from which it conducts its business or, if it is domiciled or ordinarily resident abroad, if it targets the German market in offering its services repeatedly and on a commercial basis to persons domiciled or ordinarily resident in Germany (see chapter 5.2.3.2).

This new licence requirement is meant to protect investors against risky investment schemes and to improve the integrity of the financial market. The German legislator intended to stop so-called "grey capital" by filling the gap between schemes which are not covered on a national level by the Investment Act or on an international level by the UCITS Directive.

Intentional non-compliance with the new licence requirement is a criminal offence punishable with imprisonment up to three years or a fine. Negligent non-compliance is punishable with imprisonment of up to one year or a fine.

---

[13] *"Regierungsentwurf für ein Gesetz zur Fortentwicklung des Pfandbriefrechts vom 24. September 2008"*, see chapter *"Zu Nummer 4 (§2 Abs. 6 KWG), Zu Buchstabe a"*.
http://www.bundesfinanzministerium.de/DE/BMF__Startseite/Aktuelles/Aktuelle__Gesetze/
Gesetzentwuerfe__Arbeitsfassungen/Regierungsentw__Pfandbrief__anl,templateId=raw,property=
publicationFile.pdf

The BaFin explained the new financial service of investment management in its preliminary circular 7/2009[14] and in its guidelines of 8 December 2009[15]. There is also guidance in the explanatory note by the German government to the draft bill which introduced the new financial service.[16] A service provider who is uncertain if the new licence requirement applies, may ask the BaFin to determine whether it is subject to these Banking Act provisions.

2.2.4.1.1 Focus on purchase and sale of financial instruments

For the new licence requirement to apply, the purchase and sale of financial instruments must be one of the main features of the product.

Financial instruments are defined in §1 para (11) KWG as tradable securities, money market instruments, foreign exchange, units of account and derivatives. "Securities" include shares and units in investment funds which come within the scope of the Investment Act. Investment in financial instruments may be direct or indirect, through other products which do not themselves qualify as financial instruments. It is not a requirement that the vehicle exclusively invests in financial instruments. Other assets may be purchased and sold in addition.

The new licence requirement only applies if purchase and sale of financial instruments are amongst the principal services offered. This should be the case if marketing of the financial product concentrates on the purchase and sale of financial instruments. If the purchase and the sale of financial instruments is merely an ancillary activity, there will be no investment management within the meaning of the KWG. Consequently, companies which invest in financial instruments only temporarily or, even if permanently only for liquidity or hedging purposes, do not require a licence for investment management.

---

[14] "*Rundschreiben 7/2009 (WA) zu Änderungen des Kreditwesengesetzes für Finanzdienstleistungsunternehmen – Einführung des Erlaubnistatbestandes der Anlageverwaltung, §1 Abs. 1a Satz 2 Nr. 11 KWG*", 30.03.2009.
http://www.bafin.de/nn_1451638/SharedDocs/Veroeffentlichungen/DE/Service/Rundschreiben/2009/rs__0907__wa__anlageverwaltung.html

[15] "*Merkblatt – Hinweise zum Tatbestand der Anlageverwaltung*", 08.12.2009.
http://www.bafin.de/cln_188/nn_722552/SharedDocs/Veroeffentlichungen/DE/Service/Merkblaetter/mb__091208__tatbestand__anlageverwaltung.html?__nnn=true

[16] See footnote 13.

2.2.4.1.2 Community of investors who are natural persons

The financial services must be rendered on a collective basis for a group of individual investors if they are to qualify as investment management. There should be at least two investors. No licence requirement exists if all investors are legal persons such as companies. If there is only one natural person in a community of investors, the licence requirement applies.

Unlike the financial service of portfolio management (*Finanzportfolioverwaltung*) which is rendered on a bilateral basis and requires a separate portfolio for each customer of the portfolio manager, investment management is a service which is provided on a collective basis. It is aimed at investment schemes which target the general public and involve investors in corporate models, such as *Treuhandkommandite* or *Genussrechtsbeteiligungen* (profit-sharing rights) in order to pool investors' money in financial instruments. It is irrelevant if investors participate as shareholders or limited partners in a fund vehicle or as holders of bonds, notes or certificates. The requirement that there is a community of investors does not mean that there must be a corporate relationship. It is sufficient if investor assets are jointly managed by the service provider.

The German legislator, by choosing an economic approach intended to include all types of collective investment schemes in the new licence requirement, irrespective of the precise legal relationships. The investment management activities must ultimately be designed to allow retail investors to participate in the performance of the financial instruments purchased. The economic risk should be borne by the investors. It is sufficient that investors indirectly participate in the performance of the financial instruments. The service provider may participate jointly in the development of the portfolio in addition to being paid its service fees. Risk diversification is not a requirement.

2.2.4.1.3 Investment discretion

The purchase and sale of financial instruments must be on a discretionary basis. Investment guidelines are permitted, provided that they define suitable financial instruments only generally. There is no discretion if the investment decision is tied to a fixed policy detailing the financial instruments to be purchased and sold, including as to their quantity and the timing of the transaction. The same applies to portfolios which can only be invested in predefined companies, for example feeder funds. Such investment vehicles are not required to be licensed for investment management.

There is no discretion and no licence requirement for investment management if the purchase and sale of financial instruments cannot be undertaken without the express consent of the investor. If investors have the right to veto transactions, for example if purchases and sales become effective if investors do not object, discretion is assumed and the new licence requirement applies.

The service provider is not released from the requirement to be licensed if it bestows discretionary investment decision powers upon a third party. In this respect it does not make a difference whether the investment decision is executed by such third party or the service provider.

2.2.4.2 Examples

A typical example for licensable investment management is a German limited partnership (*Kommanditgesellschaft*), which is funded by its limited partners (*Kommanditisten*) and which invests in a portfolio of shares, money market instruments and derivatives. However, it should be noted that the new licence requirement is not limited to German entities and may also capture unregulated hedge funds registered in offshore jurisdictions. If a hedge fund of this sort targets the German market, investment management is regarded as being performed in Germany and a licence will be required.

2.2.4.2.1 Private equity

Private equity funds which purchase shares in unlisted stock corporations with the ultimate goal of onselling their investments for a return in excess of the price paid, are not required to be licensed. The reason is that their portfolio strategy is not regarded as capital investment through buying and selling financial instruments, but instead is characterised as having operational influence on the target's management and business operations. This also applies when private equity funds invest in money market instruments, listed bonds or listed companies, whether for diversification or merely to hold cash, on the basis that such activity is not the main focus of the business.

It follows from the above that private equity funds fall outside the scope of the Investment Act and the Banking Act and consequently are unregulated. German private equity funds may apply to become subject to the special regimes of the Equity Investment Companies Act (*Unternehmensbeteiligungsgesetz*, UBGG) or the Act for the Promotion of Venture Capital Participations (*Wagnisbeteiligungsgesetz,* WKBG) in order to benefit from tax relief.

2.2.4.2.2 Real estate funds

Real estate funds which focus on direct real estate investment and maintain liquidity reserves or purchase financial instruments on an ongoing but ancillary basis for hedging purposes also fall outside the scope of the Banking Act, but might be subject to the Investment Act if the preconditions described in chapter 2.1.2.1. are fulfilled. The purchase of financial instruments only for hedging purposes does not constitute a licensable financial service.

2.2.4.2.3 Special purpose vehicles

Special purpose vehicles established by credit institutions to issue bonds and certificates are generally excluded from the licence requirement. This is because special purpose vehicles typically have limited discretion to take investment decisions. Usually their sales and marketing efforts do not directly target individual investors, but are mainly addressed to the relevant credit institution. For those special purpose vehicles which do fulfill the licensing conditions, the exemption of a licensed parent company in §2 para (6) no. 18 KWG may apply (see chapter 2.2.4.3.2).

2.2.4.2.4 Family offices

Family offices, i.e. companies regardless of their legal status dealing with private wealth management independent of any credit institution, fall outside the scope of the new licence requirement.[17]

2.2.4.3 Exemptions

2.2.4.3.1 Services to group companies

Enterprises which provide financial services only to their parent or subsidiary or affiliated enterprises are not deemed to be financial services institutions, and therefore do not require a financial services licence (§2 para (6) sentence 1 no. 5 KWG).

---

[17] *"BaFin Merkblatt zur Erlaubnispflicht gemäß §32 Abs. 1 KWG für Family Offices"*, 10.02.2009. http://www.bafin.de/cln_161/nn_721290/SharedDocs/Veroeffentlichungen/DE/Service/Merkblaetter/ mb__080630__familyoffices.html?__nnn=true

2.2.4.3.2 Licence of parent company

§2 para (6) no. 18 KWG excludes any enterprise from the licensing requirement if (i) it does not provide financial services other than investment management and (ii) its parent company is licensed for investment management. The German legislator took the view that the involvement of at least one regulated entity is sufficient to ensure investor protection.

The exemption in §2 para (6) no. 18 KWG extends to German subsidiaries of deposit-taking credit institutions and securities trading firms located in the EEA, provided that the parent company has a banking or financial services licence comparable to investment management as defined §1 para (1) a sentence 2 no. 11 KWG in such parent's home member state. The BaFin takes the approach that if the home regulator interprets the list of investment services and activities in Annex I, Section A to the Financial Instruments Directive (MiFID) (2004/39/EC) to include collective investment management, the BaFin will accept this interpretation. The subsidiary of the passported service provider will be allowed to provide its services, being the offering of interests in its collective investment scheme, in Germany.

§2 para (6) no. 18 KWG also excludes German subsidiaries of non-EEA parent companies which have applied to the BaFin for an exemption from the licence requirement, because the nature of their business does not require supervision, and the exemption has been granted.

2.2.4.4 Foreign investment management service providers

Foreign service providers wishing to offer collective investment management in Germany need to have a banking or financial services licence from the BaFin, unless the exemption for a licensed parent company applies (see chapter 2.2.4.3.2).

2.2.4.4.1 Licence of parent company

EEA service providers cannot benefit from an EU single market passport, because collective investment management is not expressly covered by MiFID or the Banking Consolidation Directive (2006/48/EC)[18]. However, the BaFin takes the approach that if an EEA vehicle is licensed in its home member state and provided its licence covers collective

---

[18] http://eur-lex.europa.eu/LexUriServ/LexUriServ.do?uri=OJ:L:2006:177:0001:0200:EN:PDF

investment management as interpreted by the competent home member state authority, then the view of such authority will prevail and the fund will be able to provide its services in Germany based on its EU passport.

2.2.4.4.2 Passive freedom to provide services

Another exemption to the new licence requirement is the passive freedom of services doctrine (see chapter 5.2.2.2.2). No licence under the KWG is required if the contract between the financial services provider and the customer is initiated by the customer without prior solicitation.

2.2.4.5 Securities Trading Act

§2 para (3) sentence 3 WpHG provides that investment managers are subject to the same WpHG rules as portfolio managers but unlike portfolio managers, they do not qualify as investment services enterprises (*Wertpapierdienstleistungsunternehmen*). Investment managers must comply with reporting obligations to the BaFin (§9 WpHG), how they are organised, their transparency (§§31 to 34 and 34b to 36b WpHG) and record-keeping of client orders and transactions (Article 7 and 8 of Regulation (EC) No 1287/2006[19]). The explanatory note by the German government to the draft bill which introduced the new financial service of collective investment management, states that these rules apply only to the extent they are suitable and relevant in individual cases.[20]

---

[19] "Commission regulation (EC) No 1287/2006 of 10 August 2006 implementing Directive 2004/39/EC of the European Parliament and of the Council as regards recordkeeping obligations for investment firms, transaction reporting, market transparency, admission of financial instruments to trading, and defined terms for the purposes of that Directive".
http://eur-lex.europa.eu/LexUriServ/LexUriServ.do?uri=OJ:L:2006:241:0001:0025:EN:PDF

[20] See footnote 13, see chapter "*Zu Artikel 3 (Änderung des Wertpapierhandelsgesetzes)*".

CHAPTER 3 - PRIVATE PLACEMENTS

The Investment Act provides a regulatory framework for public marketing and distribution of foreign investment funds in Germany, but not for their private placement. Consequently, there are no market access barriers for private placements of non-German investment funds. If a foreign Investment Company restricts its fund marketing and distribution to private placements, no notification needs to be made with the BaFin. Hence the boundary between public offer and private placement is important.

The following explanations apply only to the marketing and distribution of investment funds, both UCITS and non-UCITS, as defined in the Investment Act (see chapter 2.1), but not to other fund-like products which are subject to different regulatory regimes. Each marketing event needs to be judged on its own merits. In some cases it might be difficult to determine if an activity constitutes a private placement or if it crosses the line and amounts to a public offer.

In practice, private placements play a more significant role for non-UCITS than for UCITS, because UCITS with their EU passport can relatively easily gain access to the public market in Germany by filing a notification with the BaFin (see chapter 4.1). Non-UCITS on the other hand are either banned altogether from public marketing in Germany, for instance regulated single hedge funds (see chapter 2.1.2.2.2), or have to make a complex and often time-consuming registration with the BaFin before they can lawfully commence public marketing in Germany (see chapter 2.1.2.2).

3.1 Definitions

3.1.1 Public distribution, §2 para (11) sentence 1 InvG

Pursuant to §2 para (11) sentence 1 InvG, "public distribution" is defined as "marketing by way of public offering, public advertising or in a similar manner".

3.1.1.1 Reference to a specific fund

Marketing will come within the ambit of the Investment Act if it relates to a specific fund. If the marketing comprises non-specific information about foreign funds or the use only of the group name or logo, it will not amount to public distribution and will not be regulated by the Investment Act.[21] Such activity will not constitute a private placement unless it took place before the fund was offered to the investor who was the subject of the marketing.

If the investment fund is identified by name without any further information being provided, by law this constitutes private placement and not public distribution (see chapter 3.1.2.2.2).

3.1.1.2 "Offering" and "advertising" or "a similar manner"

"Offering" means any invitation to buy. The invitation does not need to be a legal offering, but it is sufficient if it is an offering only in the commercial sense.[22] Any inducement to purchase fund units, any activity drawing an investor's attention to the availability of fund units or indicating how information may be obtained about their supply is sufficient to qualify as an offering.[23] If a customer is given the opportunity to make a binding offer to purchase units which the Investment Company can subsequently accept, this activity will qualify as an offering. It is not necessary that the sale is completed. An offering may be oral with customers on the distributor's or customer's premises, by telephone, mail or e-mail, on the internet or in a newspaper.

Frequently when there is an offering there will be advertising. "Advertising" has a broader meaning and comprises any means of communication which is intended to make investors look favourably on the fund units in question.[24] Investment Companies or their distributors sometimes indirectly engage in advertising, for example by allowing journalists to report on a fund in order to advance its sale prospects.[25]

The catch-all phrase in §2 para (11) sentence 1 InvG "in a similar manner" is intended to cover new ways of marketing and distribution in case they are not already included in the words "offering" and "advertising".[26]

---

[21] Pfüller/Schmitt in Brinkhaus/Scherer, Gesetz über Kapitalanlagegesellschaften / Auslandinvestment-Gesetz, München 2003, §1 AuslInvestmG, note 15.

[22] Vahldiek in Bödecker, Handbuch Investmentrecht, Bad Soden 2007, §2, L.; Pfüller/Schmitt in Brinkhaus/Scherer, see footnote 21, §1 AuslInvestmG, note 7.

[23] Beckmann in Beckmann/Scholtz/Vollmer, Investment - Ergänzbares Handbuch für das gesamte Investmentwesen, Bielefeld, Loseblatt, supplement 9/09 - IX.09, Vol. 1, §2 InvG, note 288.

[24] Baur, Investmentgesetze, 2. Edition, Vol. 2 , Berlin 1997, § 1 AuslInvestmG, note 20; Pfüller/Schmitt in Brinkhaus/Scherer, see footnote 21, §1 AuslInvestmG, note 7.

[25] Baur, see footnote 24, § 1 AuslInvestmG, note 20.

[26] Beckmann in Beckmann/Scholtz/Vollmer, see footnote 23, supplement 9/09 - IX.09, Vol. 1, §2 InvG, note 293; Baur, see footnote 24, §1 AuslInvestmG, note 22.

3.1.1.3 "Public"

"Offering" and "advertising" need to be directed at the public in Germany.

3.1.1.3.1 In Germany

Only activities in Germany are relevant. Consequently, if German residents are solicited by an offering or advertising of fund units whilst they are outside Germany, such solicitation is irrelevant from the German regulatory perspective, provided that it is not directed into Germany.[27] If investors within Germany are targeted from abroad, for example by radio, television, newspapers, mail, e-mail or the internet, such marketing then becomes subject to German regulatory law, since it is regarded as taking place in Germany.[28] The same will apply if customer service representatives travel from outside into Germany or if the Investment Company undertakes offering and/or advertising activities from a German branch office or through a German group company or intermediary.

3.1.1.3.2 Public

The German government defined the meaning of the word "public" in its explanatory note to the draft bill of the Foreign Investment Act (*Auslandinvestment-Gesetz*) of 1968, which introduced regulation of public distribution of foreign investment funds, as an indefinite group of persons, whether natural or legal persons.[29] A group is indefinite if all individuals or the majority of them are not identified.[30] The term "public" is not defined by the number of addressees but by their being indeterminate. The distinguishing feature is qualitative not quantitative (see also chapter 3.1.2.1).[31]

Attracting the attention of the public at large is always considered to fall within the meaning of the word "public", for example by mass mailings by post or e-mail, display of marketing materials in business premises or offices which are accessible to the general public and advertisements in the press, radio, television or internet.[32]

---

[27] Baur, see footnote 24, §1 AusIInvestmG, note 23.

[28] Vahldiek in Bödecker, see footnote 22, § 2, L.

[29] *Amtliche Begründung Regierungsentwurf zum Auslandinvestment-Gesetz*, BT-Drucks. V/3494 B, Art.1 zu §1, S. 17.

[30] Vahldiek in Bödecker, see footnote 22, §2, L.

[31] Pfüller/Schmitt in Brinkhaus/Scherer, see footnote 21, §1 AusIInvestmG, note 11.

[32] Baur, see footnote 24, §1 AusIInvestmG, note 15; Beckmann in Beckmann/Scholtz/Vollmer, see footnote 23, supplement 9/09 - IX.09, Vol. 1, §2 InvG, note 311.

Public activity will start with the possibility of any one individual becoming aware of it and ends when no one could be aware of it.[33] It is irrelevant if anybody has in fact taken any notice.[34]

3.1.2 Private placement

3.1.2.1 By reverse conclusion from §2 para (11) sentence 1 InvG

"Private placement" is not defined in the Investment Act. Although the Investment Act indirectly takes note of the concept of private placement in the context of distribution of single hedge funds (§112 para (2) InvG). The definition of "public distribution" in §2 para (11) sentence 1 InvG and its suggested interpretation, however, allow for the conclusion that a private placement must be limited to a definite and finite group of persons, whether natural or legal persons.

The BaFin's predecessor, the *Bundesaufsichtsamt für den Wertpapierhandel* (BAWe), in an announcement on 6 September 1999 explained the private placement rules under the Sales Prospectus Act (*Verkaufsprospektgesetz*)[35]. This announcement is still used as guidance for the private placement of investment funds.[36] Whereas "public offering" is defined as an offering for sale to an undefined number of persons who are not yet known to the offeror, "private placement" is defined as an offer made to a limited number of private and/or institutional investors who do not require the protection of a registered prospectus. A limited number of addressees will exist if they are previously and individually known to the offeror and selectively approached on the basis of their individual characteristics. The BaFin considers a placement in principle to be private only if all recipients of the offer have an existing investment relationship with the offeror. As a result, private placements are restricted to investors with whom the Investment Company already has an existing customer relationship and the investor has either expressed interest or may be expected to be interested in receiving unsolicited investment recommendations of the specific kind contemplated by the private placement.

---

[33] Baur, see footnote 24, §1 AuslInvestmG, note 15; Pfüller/Schmitt in Brinkhaus/Scherer, see footnote 21, §1 AuslInvestmG, note 15.

[34] Pfüller/Schmitt in Brinkhaus/Scherer, see footnote 21, §1 AuslInvestmG, note 15.

[35] *Bekanntmachung des Bundesaufsichtsamtes für den Wertpapierhandel (BAWe) zum Wertpapier-Verkaufsprospektgesetz (Verkaufsprospektgesetz)*, 06.09.1999.
http://www.bafin.de/cln_109/nn_721290/SharedDocs/Downloads/DE/Service/Aufsichtsrecht/bek99__01,templateId=raw,property=publicationFile.pdf/bek99_01.pdf

[36] Pfüller/Schmitt in Brinkhaus/Scherer, see footnote 21, §1 AuslInvestmG, note 12.

For regulated single hedge funds, the German legislator explained in its introduction to §112 para (2) InvG that only private placements are permitted, so that "not everyone, for example small retail investors, invests into single hedge funds, but only certain private investors who specifically look for an investment into single hedge funds and in respect of whom it may be assumed that they have sufficient knowledge of the risks and the necessary assets".[37] These principles might be applied to private placements of other types of funds. Active soliciting should be limited to existing clients who the Investment Company in good faith assumes are sufficiently knowledgeable to be able to ascertain the risks of the investment and who have sufficient assets to diversify their risks when investing in the fund. Indiscriminate solicitation of all existing customers could be regarded as a public offering. Although the BaFin does not limit the number of addressees, it has indicated that it would interpret a smaller number as an indication of a limited group, provided that the above conditions are satisfied.

It is often the case that the Investment Company will not have existing customers in Germany. The definition of private placements should, therefore, be extended to clients of the asset management group to which the Investment Company belongs, and also to clients of a limited number of independent distributors with whom the Investment Company cooperates.[38] Otherwise newly established funds would be excluded from attracting investors in Germany by private placements, even though private placements specified in §2 (11) sentence 2 InvG refer without exception to all investment funds.

It is obviously important that an Investment Company should only choose reliable partners when investment units are privately placed through independent distributors. The Investment Company should take precautionary measures to prevent distributors from offering shares indiscriminately to their own customers in a manner which is inconsistent with the above private placement principles.[39] Distributors should be contractually bound to adhere strictly to the private placement rules (see chapter 3). The Investment Company should also monitor its distributors so that no public distribution takes place.

---

[37] *Deutscher Bundestag, Bericht des Finanzausschusses (7. Ausschuss) Bundesdrucksache 15/1944 vom 5.11.2003 zu dem Gesetzentwurf der Bundesregierung – Drucksachen 15/1553, 15/1671 – zu § 112 Abs. 2 InvG.*
http://dipbt.bundestag.de/doc/btd/15/019/1501944.pdf

[38] Vahldiek in Bödecker, see footnote 22, *Vorbemerkung zu InvG* §§121-127 B.

[39] See chapter 3.4 for disclaimers.

When a new customer relationship is established, private placement becomes public distribution. This also applies if fund units are sold to existing customers who intend to resell the units in Germany.[40]

If an investor on its own initiative approaches the Investment Company or its distributor with a request for information without having been solicited, the Investment Company is permitted to provide information about its funds and to sell fund units to the investor without engaging in public distribution.

3.1.2.2 §2 (11) sentence 2 InvG

The Investment Act, since being amended on 28 December 2007, in §2 para (11) sentence 2 introduced certain exemptions which, even though public distribution is broadly defined in sentence 1, are deemed not to be a public distribution and as a result will qualify as a private placement:

3.1.2.2.1 Institutional investors

➢   Investment units are offered exclusively to German credit or financial services institutions (§1 Abs. 1b KWG), insurance companies regulated by private or public law, investment companies or investment stock corporations, non-German investment companies and their management companies, pension funds and their management companies (§2 para (11) sentence 2, no. 1 InvG).

The German legislator in its explanatory note[41] to the draft bill which introduced sentence 2 to §2 para (11) took the position that only private investors need regulatory protection under the Investment Act. This is why if foreign investment units are offered to even a large number of institutional investors, none of whom is an existing customer of the Investment Company, there is no need to consider this offering as a public distribution in order to trigger the regulatory protection of the Investment Act.

Institutional investors must either be end investors or intend to resell the units exclusively to other institutional investors as end investors. If units are offered to an institutional

---

[40]   Baur, see footnote 24, §1 AuslInvestmG, note 18.

[41]   *Deutscher Bundestag Drucksache 16/5576, 16. Wahlperiode, 11.06.2007, Gesetzentwurf der Bundesregierung, Entwurf eines Gesetzes zur Änderung des Investmentgesetzes und zur Anpassung anderer Vorschriften (Investmentänderungsgesetz)*, zu §2 para (11) sentence 2.
http://dipbt.bundestag.de/dip21/btd/16/055/1605576.pdf

investor who plans to resell them to private investors, this will be regarded public distribution by the foreign Investment Company.

3.1.2.2.2 Reference to fund by name

➢ Investment funds are mentioned by name only (§2 para (11) sentence 2, no. 2 InvG).

This exemption is relevant if, for example in the fund documentation the Investment Company is by EU law (Schedule A, 1.3 of the UCITS Directive) or home state law required to mention other funds which it also manages.

3.1.2.2.3 Publication of issue and redemption prices

➢ Together with the fund name issue and redemption prices are published (§2 para (11) sentence 2, no.3 InvG).

References to an investment fund by name and publications of issue and redemption prices do not necessitate regulatory protection for private investors. Even though such information may attract new investors to the fund, the German legislator regards it as too general and abstract to qualify as public distribution.

3.1.2.2.4 Umbrella funds

➢ Umbrella fund sales documentation comprising full and simplified sales prospectus, annual and subsequent semi-annual reports, and constitutive documents, contain information on sub-funds which are not required to be notified for public distribution in Germany, provided that each document shows the warning notice in the way prescribed by the Investment Act (§2 para (11) sentence 2, no. 4 InvG) (see chapter 4.3.3.3).

If marketing material for sub-funds of an umbrella fund which are permitted to be publicly marketed in Germany contains information about other sub-funds which are not notified to the BaFin, public distribution of the marketing materials is unlawful to the extent the distribution relates to the non-permitted sub-funds, unless the exemption set out in §2 para (11) sentence 2 no. 4 InvG applies.

Before the exemption for umbrella funds was introduced into the Investment Act, German sales documentation for sub-funds in respect of which notice for public distribution in Germany had been given to the BaFin, was not permitted to contain any information about other sub-funds of which such notice had not been given to the BaFin. The result was that the BaFin only processed whole umbrella notifications in respect of which notice for public distribution in Germany had been given to it covering all the sub-funds, even if the Investment Company intended actively to market only some of them.

3.1.2.2.5 Publication of bases of taxation

➢ The bases of taxation are published pursuant to §5 InvStG (§2 para (11) sentence 2, no. 5 InvG).

If the Investment Company fulfills the calculation and publication requirements pursuant to §5 InvStG (the principle of tax transparency, see chapter 6.3), its investors will benefit from a more advantageous tax treatment than the punitive lump-sum taxation which would otherwise apply. By introducing this safe-harbour, investment funds can opt to satisfy the tax transparency rules without being admitted for public distribution. This allows those investment funds which are intended for private placement only or which cannot be registered for public sale, to allow their investors to benefit from the more advantageous tax treatment as well.

3.1.2.2.6 Derivatives based upon investment funds

➢ Information on investment funds is included in prospectuses for issues of securities or other non-security investments as part of statutory minimum information requirements pursuant to §7 WpPG or §8g VerkprospektG (§2 para (11) sentence 2, no. 6 InvG).

This exemption is crucial for derivative products related to investment funds, especially certificates linked to hedge funds or fund indices. There had been prolonged uncertainty about how to reconcile seemingly conflicting requirements between the Securities Prospectus Act and the Sales Prospectus Act which require derivative product prospectuses to include information on investment funds which serve as reference assets, and on the other hand the Investment Act which could be interpreted as prohibiting publication of such information as unlawful public marketing if the underlying investment funds were not registered with the BaFin.

3.1.2.2.2.7 Listing on a stock exchange

➤ Foreign investment units may be admitted for trading on the Regulated Market (*regulierter Markt*) or introduced into the Regulated Market or Regulated Unofficial Market (*Freiverkehr*) of a German stock exchange, provided that only those announcements prescribed by the exchange are made in respect of the fund and no other public marketing of units takes place (§2 para (11) sentence 2, no.7 InvG).

3.2 The internet

Offering and advertising fund units on the internet through generally accessible websites constitutes public distribution. It will take place in Germany if any part of the website is directly addressed to German investors. The country where the information is uploaded or where the server is positioned will not affect this conclusion, provided that investors in Germany are targeted.[42] The BaFin issued administrative guidelines on 2 June 1998 on distribution of foreign investment units on the internet[43], which followed the approach of the BaFin's predecessor, the *Bundesaufsichtsamt für das Kreditwesen* (BAKred). An overall assessment should be made by considering the particulars of each website.

3.2.1 Websites in the German language

A strong indication that German investors amongst others are targeted is the use of the German language. Information about foreign investment units on German internet sites will typically amount to a public offering in Germany. There may be exceptions if the website is clearly only directed at investors in German-speaking jurisdictions other than Germany. Website providers from such jurisdictions should design their websites so as not to attract German customers and not advertise fund units tailored for the German market, to avoid unlawful public distribution in Germany. The pages of the website should not contain any reference to Germany, for example information about German taxation, legal conditions or offers of services specifically for customers resident in Germany, including

---

[42] *Bekanntmachung des Bundesaufsichtsamtes für den Wertpapierhandel (BAWe) zum Wertpapier-Verkaufsprospektgesetz (Verkaufsprospektgesetz)*, 06.09.1999, note 2. b), see footnote 35.

[43] Öffentlicher Vertrieb ausländischer Investmentanteile im Internet (deutsch-englisch), Bundesaufsichtsamt für das Kreditwesen (BAKred), 02.06.1998.
http://www.bafin.de/cln_109/nn_722552/SharedDocs/Artikel/DE/Unternehmen/Fonds/Investmentfonds/ba__980602.html?__nnn=true

paying agent services. An express disclaimer that the units are not publicly marketed or distributed in Germany should be displayed prominently on the website.[44]

Whether German resident investors should be allowed to buy units over the internet which would otherwise not be permitted for public distribution in Germany is a matter of controversy. According to the BaFin's announcement of 6 September 1999[45], the offeror must ensure that investors in Germany will not be able to purchase the securities.[46] In later publications[47] the BaFin emphasises that persons and enterprises resident in Germany have the right on their own initiative to request services from a foreign provider. Based on this principle, the acceptance of unsolicited purchase orders (passive freedom to provide services, see chapter 5.2.2.2.2) should be allowed.[48]

3.2.2 Websites in other languages

Websites containing information in languages other than German are not regarded as giving rise to public offerings in Germany, so long as they clearly do not aim to attract investors in Germany. To avoid unlawful public marketing, such websites must not contain any reference to Germany. If the website for example mentions a contact address in Germany, special information for German resident investors or otherwise indicates that the website could also be directed at investors who are resident in Germany, any of these factors will amount to public marketing in Germany irrespective of the website's language or if the website contains a disclaimer.

3.2.3 Websites intended for distribution of foreign investment funds in Germany

Websites which target the German market must be designed in accordance with applicable marketing rules (see chapter 6.1 and 6.2).

---

[44] For a sample disclaimer in the English language see Pfüller/Schmitt in Brinkhaus/Scherer, see footnote 21, §1 AuslInvestmG, note 19.

[45] *Bekanntmachung des Bundesaufsichtsamtes für den Wertpapierhandel (BAWe) zum Wertpapier-Verkaufsprospektgesetz (Verkaufsprospektgesetz)*, 6.09.1999, note 2. b), see footnote 35.

[46] For this view see Pfüller/Schmitt in Brinkhaus/Scherer, see footnote 21, §1 AuslInvestmG, note 20.

[47] *Merkblatt - Hinweise zur Erlaubnispflicht nach § 32 Abs. 1 KWG in Verbindung mit § 1 Abs. 1 und Abs. 1a KWG von grenzüberschreitend betriebenen Bankgeschäften und/oder grenzüberschreitend erbrachten Finanzdienstleistungen*, 01.04.2005.
http://www.bafin.de/cln_109/nn_722552/SharedDocs/Veroeffentlichungen/DE/Service/Merkblaetter/mb__050400__grenzueberschreitend.html?__nnn=true

[48] Vahldiek in Bödecker, see footnote 22, §1 D. III. 2.

The website should be in the German language to the extent that it is directed at investors resident in Germany and it contains information about funds which are permitted to be publicly marketed in Germany.[49] This is because the Investment Act requires that all publications relating to foreign investment funds must be in the German language (§ 123 InvG). Information about funds which are only privately placed does not need to be in the German language, because the Investment Act does not apply to private placements (see chapter 3.3).

If such websites contain information about funds which are permitted to be publicly marketed in Germany and about other funds, precautionary measures should be taken to avoid unlawful public marketing. The safest approach is to technically restrict access of internet users who do not qualify for private placements of those other funds, being users who are not institutional investors or existing customers as described above (see chapters 3.1.2.1 and 3.1.2.2.1).

3.2.4 References to websites in printed marketing material

It is frequently the case that prospectuses, reports or other marketing material relating to foreign investment funds which are permitted for public marketing in Germany contain references to websites where further information on the funds may be obtained. The website provider in these circumstances should ensure that the website does not contain information on any other funds which are not permitted for public marketing in Germany or that access to such information is restricted as described in chapter 3.2.3 above, because otherwise it might be construed as unlawful public marketing.

3.3 Applicable rules

The Investment Act does not regulate private placements of foreign investment funds, except for regulated hedge funds (§ 1 sentence 1 no. 3 InvG), nor is the private placement of foreign investment funds subject to the Sales Prospectus Act (*VerkaufsprospekG*), the Securities Sales Prospectus Act (WpPG) or other regulatory law. Private placements might, however, be subject to other German laws, in particular competition law (see chapter 6.2), tax law (see chapter 6.3) and as summarised below, private law (see chapters 3.3.2 to 3.3.5).

---

[49] Schmies in Beckmann/Scholtz/Vollmer, see footnote 23, supplement 5/05 - X.05, Vol. 2, § 123 InvG, notes 7 and 8.

3.3.1 Hedge funds and funds of hedge funds

§121 para (3) InvG prescribes rules for the sale of hedge funds and funds of hedge funds within the meaning of §112 and §113 InvG (see chapters 2.1.2.2.2 and 2.1.2.2.3). If the investor is a private person, before conclusion of the sales contract the vendor, i.e. the Investment Company and the distributors and intermediaries it has instructed[50], must deliver the current prospectus, the constitutive documents and the most recent annual and subsequent semi-annual report to the investor free of charge and without prior request. In the context of distance contracts (see chapter 7.2.2), prior delivery of fund documentation can be achieved by making their download from the internet to the investor's computer a compulsory prerequisite to purchase the units.[51]

A sales contract with a private person must be in writing to be valid, i.e. bearing a personal signature or notarised hand signature (§126 para (1) BGB). A qualifying electronic signature in accordance with the German Electronic Signatures Act is also permitted (§126a para (1) BGB).

Prior to concluding the sales contract, pursuant to §117 para (2) and (3) InvG the private investor must be expressly warned about the risks inherent in the fund. The prospectus must contain the following risk warnings in a prominent place and typographically highlighted:

> **"Warning by the Federal Minister of Finance: Investors in this investment fund must be prepared and able to sustain losses of the capital invested up to a total loss."**

If a prime broker holds the assets of the fund in custody the above risk warning must be supplemented as follows:

> **"The assets of this investment fund are not held in custody by a custodian bank in whole or in part."**

If the prime broker has its seat outside Germany the above risk warning must indicate this fact and refer to the fact that the prime broker is not subject to state supervision by the BaFin.

---

[50] OLG Hamm, Urteil v. 31.1.2000, Az. 31 U 167/97; Schödermeier/Baltzer in Brinkhaus/Scherer, see footnote 21, §19 KAGG, note 15.

[51] Schmies in Beckmann/Scholtz/Vollmer, see footnote 23, supplement 5/05 – X.05, Vol. 1, §121 InvG, note 24; Vahldiek in Bödecker, see footnote 22, §121 D.

If the fund is closed-end, the prospectus must include an express and typographically highlighted warning that the investor may not at any time demand to redeem his units and be paid out that portion of the pool of assets which represents his units.

If there is a dispute about whether a risk warning has been given the burden of proof lies with the seller.

The rules set out in this chapter do not apply to the acquisition of units under financial portfolio management within the meaning of §1 para (1a) no. 3 KWG. If units are acquired at regular intervals under an investment savings plan, these rules only apply to the first purchase order (§121 para (3a) InvG).

Investors in foreign hedge funds may be entitled to claim compensation under §127 InvG if information contained in the sales prospectus is inaccurate or incomplete (see chapter 7.3.1).[52]

3.3.2 Contract law

The contractual relationship between an Investment Company and its investors who habitually reside in Germany is governed by German contract law, provided that German law applies under private international law. This is usually not the case (see chapter 7.3.3.1.1).

If German contract law applies, the Investment Company has an advisory duty to investors arising out of the customer relationship. Private placements need not be supported by a prospectus or other written information, but private law principles of good faith and equity require that an existing prospectus is provided to investors and investors are informed about specific risks in an appropriate manner before they purchase fund units.[53] Culpable breaches of such private law duties may lead to investor compensation claims, for example on the basis of breach of a pre-contractual or contractual obligation to disclose information or advise the investor and prospectus liability (see chapter 7.3.3).

3.3.3 Consumer protection

German consumer protection law applies under private international law whenever fund units are marketed to consumers by foreign distributors in Germany (see chapter 7.2.1).

---

[52] Vahldiek in Bödecker, see footnote 22, *Vorbemerkung zu InvG* §§ 121-127, C. I. 3.
[53] Vahldiek in Bödecker, see footnote 22, *Vorbemerkung zu InvG* §§121-127 C.

3.3.3.1 Information duties

§§312 et seq BGB impose information duties on entrepreneurs. No derogation is permitted which would disadvantage consumers (see chapter 7.2).

3.3.3.2 Revocation rights

Natural persons (consumers) who buy fund units from the Investment Company for purposes other than their trade, business or profession have a right of revocation if the transaction is a doorstep transaction (§312 BGB). A doorstep transaction is when a contract is entered into between an entrepreneur and a consumer, whose subject matter is performance for remuneration and which the consumer has been induced to enter into:

1. by oral negotiations at the consumer's place of employment or in a private home;

2. at a social or marketing event hosted by the entrepreneur or third party, which occurred at least in part for the benefit of the entrepreneur; or

3. following an impromptu approach on public transport or in a location generally accessible to the public.

The consumer has the right to revoke a doorstep transaction under §355 BGB.

The consumer's right of revocation will not arise in the case of 1. above, if the oral negotiations which lead to the transaction take place at the consumer's request or if performance of the transaction takes place immediately and is paid for when the negotiations conclude and provided that the entrepreneur's remuneration does not exceed EUR40.00 (§312 para (3) BGB).

The revocation must be communicated in writing to the Investment Company within two weeks of the consumer having been expressly informed in writing of the right to revoke in accordance with §360 para (1) BGB.[54] The consumer does not have to give any reasons for revoking the transaction (§355 para (1) BGB).

The Investment Company must inform the consumer of the following matters: the name and address of the person to whom revocation should be made, when the two week time period for the revocation starts and expires, that the consumer does not have to give reasons and the revocation must be in writing (§355 para (2) sentence 1 BGB). If the consumer is informed of his right to revoke in such terms after the contract has been entered into, the revocation period will be one month from when the consumer receives all such information about his right to revoke (§355 para (1) sentence 2 BGB). The right to revoke expires not later than six months after conclusion of the contract, unless the consumer has not been properly informed of his right of revocation (§355 para (3) BGB).

3.3.4 Rescission rights (*Anfechtungsrechte*)

In addition to the right of revocation contained in §312 BGB, the German Civil Code provides investors with certain rescission rights. However, as regards foreign Investment Companies, German investors only benefit from these rights if under German conflict of law rules German contract law applies to the legal relationship between investor and company (see chapter 7.1.2). This is usually not the case (see chapter 7.3.3.1.1).

3.3.5 Tort

If the Investment Company is in breach of private placement rules and publicly markets investment funds which have not been notified to the BaFin it may be liable for damages under the German law of tort.

---

[54]
§360 BGB in the version of 11.06.2010 (English convenience translation):
(1) The instructions on the revocation right must be clearly stated and explain to the investor his basic rights in accordance with the exigencies of the relevant communication method. They have to contain the following
1. Notice about the revocation right
2. Advice that the revocation declaration does not need to provide reasons and that the revocation can be declared in text form or by return consignment of the subject of the contract within the revocation period
3. The name and deliverable address of the addressee of the revocation declaration and
4. Advice on the length and start date of the revocation period as well as on the adequateness of the timely dispatch of the revocation declaration or return consignment within the revocation period.

Under the EU Regulation on the law which applies to non-contractual obligations[55], tortious liability derives from the law of the country in which the damage occurs (see chapter 7.3.3.2). For economic and financial loss, damage occurs where the relevant assets of the investor are situated.[56]

Under §823 para (2) BGB, a plaintiff can claim damages against another person for loss due to intentional or negligent breach of a *Schutzgesetz*, an obligation or prohibition laid down in another part of the German legal regime, provided that the *Schutzgesetz* has as its purpose the protection of individual persons and the plaintiff is a protected person.

Notification requirements[57] for public distribution of investment funds and information duties in §121 para (1) InvG[58] (see chapter 6.1) are protective provisions (*Schutzgesetz*) within the meaning of §823 para (2) BGB. This should also apply to duties to provide information and risk warnings pursuant to §121 para (3) InvG for the private placement of hedge funds (see chapter 3.3.1). Consequently, if fund units are sold publicly in Germany without being notified to the BaFin, or if statutory information or risk warnings which attach to hedge funds are not complied with, the investor may be entitled to tortious damages pursuant to §823 para (2) BGB.

If a protective provision has objectively been infringed, it is presumed that the defendant's conduct was culpable. The burden of proof is on the defendant to show that the breach was not caused by circumstances within its sphere of responsibility and the plaintiff does not have to prove fault on the part of the defendant.[59] Provided that all further requirements to prove a tortious claim are satisfied, the investor has to be put into the same position as if it had not purchased the units. The limitation period is three years.

---

[55] "Regulation (EC) No 864/2007 of the European Parliament and of the Council of 11 July 2007 on the law applicable to non-contractual obligations (Rome II)".
http://eur-lex.europa.eu/LexUriServ/LexUriServ.do?uri=OJ:L:2007:199:0040:0049:EN:PDF

[56] Palandt, Bürgerliches Gesetzbuch, 69. ed., München 2010, EG 40, note 5.

[57] Bundesgerichtshof, Urteil vom 13.09.2004, Az. II ZR 276/02.
http://juris.bundesgerichtshof.de/cgi-bin/rechtsprechung/document.py?Gericht=bgh&Art=en&sid=d4ba2839d07ce83411dc4aa5e324215d&nr=30522&pos=1&anz=10
OLG Celle, Urteil vom 25.04.2007, Az. 9 U 122/06.
http://www.jurion.de/login/login.jsp?goToUrl=../urteil/262811.html&docid=1-262811
Baur in Assmann/Schütze Handbuch des Kapitalanlagerechts, 3 Aufl. München 2007, §20, note 378

[58] OLG Hamm, Urteil v. 31.1.2000, Az. 31 U 167/97; Baur, see footnote 24, § 19 KAGG, notes 13, 21; Schödermeier/Baltzer in Brinkhaus/Scherer, see footnote 21, §19 KAGG, note 17.

[59] Palandt, see footnote 56, §823 note 81.

3.4 Preparation of private placement information material

If an investment fund is distributed to customers who qualify for private placements, the Investment Company should take precautions to prevent printed information material from being forwarded to investors who do not qualify for private placements. Any printed information about a fund which is not permitted to be distributed publicly in Germany should contain a disclaimer on its front page that the fund is not admitted for public distribution in Germany and may only be acquired by way of private placement, and must not be marketed publicly.[60] The information material should clearly be marked as confidential, for internal use only and not for public use. This also applies to any information material which can be viewed on and/or printed from the internet.

The Investment Company should keep a record of who receives information and what material they have been provided with, in order to evidence that information has been disseminated only within the private placement rules. If properly selected private placement intermediaries or customers unlawfully forward private placement materials to members of the public, the Investment Company runs the risk of being held responsible by the BaFin for public distribution. In this situation, a disclaimer might not provide a sufficient defence. A disclaimer might, however, still be useful for the Investment Company to make a claim against the intermediary or customer who circulated the information in contravention of the terms of the disclaimer, if it suffers financial loss because of the unlawful public marketing.

---

[60] For a sample disclaimer in the English language see Pfüller/Schmitt in Brinkhaus/Scherer, see footnote 21, §1 AuslInvestmG, note 19.

CHAPTER 4 - PUBLIC DISTRIBUTION OF UCITS

4.1 UCITS III notification procedure

The intention of the UCITS Directive is to facilitate the distribution of investment fund products within the EU by introducing a passport for UCITS funds based on mutual recognition. The UCITS Directive allows the units of a UCITS to be publicly distributed in any Member State without seeking authorisation in the Host Member State, provided that the notification requirements of the UCITS Directive as implemented in the respective Host Member State have been fulfilled.

In Germany and other Member States, due to divergent national practice in the enforcement of UCITS law, these notification requirements had developed into a de facto registration procedure, which could be very time-consuming and costly for the UCITS and ultimately its investors. These were the findings of CESR, which in June 2006 published the *"CESR guidelines to simplify the notification procedure of UCITS"* (CESR Guidelines)[61].

With effect from 28 December 2007, the German Investment Act was modified amongst others in order more closely to reflect the UCITS Directive. In addition, the BaFin issued guidelines for the notification of UCITS for public distribution in Germany (BaFin Guidelines) and most recently updated the guidelines on 18 March 2009[62] to align its administrative practice with CESR's recommendations. As a result of these legislative and administrative actions, the notification of UCITS for public distribution in Germany follows standardised rules adopted across the EU, complemented by distribution rules specific to Germany to the extent allowed for in the UCITS Directive. Whilst this should provide for straightforward notification procedures based on European standards, in practice administrative hurdles sometimes need to be overcome before a UCITS can be offered to the German public.

The aim of UCITS IV is to demolish administrative barriers contained within the current notification procedure and facilitate quicker EEA market access for UCITS by introducing a regulator to regulator procedure. A UCITS intending to market its units in another Member State will inform its Home Member State Authority accordingly and send it the notification documents. The notification letter should include information on the

---

[61] http://www.cesr-eu.org/data/document/06_120b.pdf

[62] http://www.bafin.de/cln_171/SharedDocs/Downloads/DE/Service/Merkblaetter/mb_080107_
anzeigeinvest,templateId=raw,property=publicationFile.pdf/mb_080107_anzeigeinvest.pdf

arrangements for marketing units of the UCITS in the Host Member State and attach the latest version of the constitutive documents, prospectus, key investor information and where appropriate, latest annual report and subsequent semi-annual report, if applicable accompanied by translations. The Home Member State Authority will check that the file is complete. If it is, no later than 10 working days after the date of receipt of the notification letter and the complete documentation, the Home Member State Authority will transmit the file to the Host Member State Authority, attesting that the UCITS fulfills its obligations under the UVITS IV Directive. Following such transmission, the UCITS Host Member State cannot object to a UCITS established in another Member State having access to its market or challenge the authorisation given by the other Member State. The Host Member State Authority cannot request additional documents, certificates or information. When the file has been transmitted to the Host Member State Authority, the Home Member State Authority will immediately notify the UCITS. From the date of such notification, the UCITS will be permitted to access the market of the Host Member State.

The following explains the procedures under UCITS III.

4.1.1 Notification to the BaFin

In Germany, the Management Company notifies the BaFin as the competent Host Member State Authority of its intention to market a non-domestic UCITS publicly. The notification procedure is governed by §§130 et seq InvG. How the BaFin administers the notification procedure is explained in the BaFin Guidelines. Further information about practical issues such as the preparation of documentation or shareholder information can be found in the BaFin FAQs which set out current BaFin practice and which can be updated by the BaFin from time to time in order to reflect changes.

4.1.2 Umbrella funds and unit classes

The Investment Act now expressly provides, in line with Guideline 9 of the CESR Guidelines, for notification of only part of the sub-funds under one umbrella-fund. Only sub-funds which are intended for active public marketing in Germany need to be notified to the BaFin. Other sub-funds which will not be offered to the German public but might still be offered by private placement (see chapter 3), need not be notified to the BaFin.

Unit classes within the same fund are treated differently from sub-funds under the same umbrella, because the fund's notification to the BaFin automatically extents to all unit classes which exist at the time of the notification or which are created at a later date, provided that the fund is already cleared for public marketing in Germany. As regards unit classes which are created at a later date, the Management Company needs to inform the BaFin about the creation of a new unit class by filing updated fund documentation which includes the additional unit classes (see chapter 4.4.1).

4.1.3 Incomplete notification

It is crucial for a successful notification that the notification file is complete and contains all required information and documents.

The BaFin confirms the date of receipt of the notification file in writing within four weeks of the filing (§132 para (3) sentence 1 InvG). In its letter of confirmation, the BaFin provides the fund with a reference number, which should be stated in all subsequent correspondence.

If the notification file is incomplete, the BaFin requires missing information and documents to be submitted.

If such requests are minor, the BaFin may in its discretion ask for additional or amended information or documentation to be provided within four weeks of the filing, and will upon receipt of any missing or incorrect item still confirm receipt of a complete notification thereby setting the waiting period running (see chapter 4.1.4) and in order not to delay public marketing.

If the BaFin makes a significant request, the Management Company must submit a supplementary filing to the BaFin within six months of submission of the original notification, counted from the date of receipt as indicated in the BaFin's first confirmation letter or within six months of the last supplementary filing counted from the date of receipt as indicated in the BaFin's last confirmation letter (§132 para (3) sentences 2 and 3 InvG).

After any such deadline has passed and the requested documents or information have not been filed in time, prohibition of public marketing of the fund becomes operative by law without any administrative BaFin order.[63] The Management Company is then at liberty to file another notification with the BaFin for the same fund as soon as it has collected the missing documents or information. The BaFin fee per fund notification (see chapter

---

[63]   Schmies in Beckmann/Scholtz/Vollmer, see footnote 23, supplement 1/07 – I.07, Vol. 2, §132, note 31.

4.3.4.2) will have to be paid for a second time and the deadlines set out above will start running again.

In order to shorten the time and effort the BaFin spends on any fund notification, the BaFin strongly disapproves of piecemeal filings, i.e. documents being filed one by one, and urges applicants to submit only when all documents have been finalised. Investment management companies wishing to gain good standing with the BaFin should note these expectations. There is no advantage to making a piecemeal filing, since the waiting period (see chapter 4.1.4) without exception runs from when the last document and information has been submitted to the BaFin.

4.1.4 Complete notification and two months waiting period

Once the BaFin has confirmed the date of receipt of the complete notification, public marketing of the fund may start at the earliest two months after the confirmed date of receipt (§133 para (1) sentence 1 InvG), unless the BaFin notifies a prior start date (§133 para (1) sentence 2 InvG). The BaFin states the specific date for commencement of public marketing in its confirmation letter.

During this two months notification period, the BaFin has the power to prohibit public marketing for the reasons set out in 4.1.5 below. If the BaFin does not prohibit public marketing during such waiting period, the Management Company is permitted to commence public marketing on the date set out in the confirmation letter without further notice. The BaFin will not issue any other written statement.

The Investment Act now empowers the BaFin, consistent with Guideline 5 of the CESR Guidelines, to shorten the two months period if the BaFin's review of the file has been finalised and there is no reason not to allow commencement of public marketing (§133 para (1) sentence 2 InvG). Depending on the quality of the filing and subject to capacity at the BaFin to review the file for its formal completeness and in relation to material issues, the BaFin regularly shortens the waiting period, often substantially.

The BaFin will inform the Management Company in writing if the waiting period is shortened. Typically, the BaFin will only issue one letter within four weeks of the filing confirming formal completeness and that no material issues hinder immediate commencement of public marketing. Accordingly, public distribution may start upon receipt of such BaFin letter, which is often considerably earlier than four weeks after the filing.

4.1.5 Prohibition of public marketing before end of the waiting period

If the Management Company starts public marketing or distribution of a UCITS in Germany without first submitting its notification for public marketing to the BaFin, or if it files a notification but commences public marketing prior to the expiry of the waiting period, the BaFin will prohibit further public marketing of the fund in Germany (§133 para (3) no. 1 InvG). The Management Company is not allowed to notify its intention to market such fund publicly in Germany again until one year has passed from the date of the prohibition (§133 para (5) InvG). Contravention of the BaFin's prohibition order is an administrative offence carrying a fine of up to EUR 100,000 (see chapter 4.5.2.3.3). Objections by the Management Company against the prohibition order and taking action to set it aside (see chapter 4.5.2.3.1) do not prevent the prohibition being effective.

If a notification filing has been submitted and the Management Company observes the waiting period, in limited circumstances the BaFin will prohibit commencement of public marketing before the end of the notification period or thereafter, but before the Management Company commences public distribution of the fund units. The circumstances in which the BaFin will make such an order are as follows (§133 para (2) InvG):

- the Management Company does not properly submit the notification to the BaFin, and the BaFin has to determine if as a result the notification is defective. If the BaFin does so determine, it will prohibit public marketing. It may be, however, that the notification is merely incomplete and can be cured by a supplementary filing (see chapter 4.1.3). In practice, this seems to be the BaFin's preferred course of action;

- the intended mode of public distribution contravenes provisions of German law other than the basic rules of the UCITS Directive as implemented in the Investment Act, for example competition law, tax law or banking and financial services law, in particular when distributors do not have necessary banking or financial services licences or EU passports (see chapter 5); or

- the Management Company does not appoint a German paying and information agent or does not name the respective agent(s) in the simplified and full prospectus (see chapters 4.2, 4.3.2.3.2 and 4.3.2.4.2) or does not fulfil other notification requirements in the prospectuses referring to umbrella funds (see chapter 4.3.3.3).

If the BaFin after a summary examination considers that any of the above circumstances might exist and that the Management Company can remedy the situation, it will notify the Management Company. This notification suspends the two months notification period. A formal objection by the Management Company against the suspension will not cause the two months notification period to start again (§133 para (1) sentences 3 and 4 InvG). The notification period will continue to run once the BaFin notifies the Management Company that the reason for the suspension has ceased to exist. By law after the cause of the suspension has been remedied by the Management Company, the BaFin has to make this notification without undue delay.

If the Management Company does not remedy the issues which caused the suspension, by written order the BaFin will prohibit public marketing of the fund. The two months notification period will not be revived by objections against or actions to set aside the prohibition (see chapter 4.5.2.3.3). However, the Management Company may file another notification with the BaFin for the same fund as soon as it has remedied the situation. In such circumstances the BaFin's fee (see chapter 4.3.4.2) will have to be paid for a second time and the deadlines set out above will start running again.

4.2 Paying and information agent in Germany

4.2.1 Paying agent

Before it notifies the fund to the BaFin for public marketing, the Management Company must nominate at least one German credit institution or German branch of a foreign credit institution as the fund's paying agent (§131 sentence 1 InvG).

The paying agent has two functions: first, it ensures that payments to German unitholders can be made and second, that redemptions and conversions of units can be processed through a German institution.

In practice, the Management Company and the paying agent on occasion agree that unitholders can subscribe for units and make payments to the fund through the paying agent, although this is not required by the Investment Act.

If payments are made from the fund to unitholders, the paying agent must ensure that the unitholders receive the payments without undue delay. The paying agent opens an account for the fund through which payments are settled. The Management Company has to maintain a credit balance in this account sufficient to enable the paying agent to effect payments.

Unitholders are entitled to payment in cash, by cheque or wire transfer to their bank accounts[64]. Although the Management Company is obliged to appoint a German paying agent, the unitholders are under no obligation to make use of this facility, but are free to receive payments and make redemptions or conversions directly through the Management Company or its German or foreign distributors.

4.2.2 Information agent

In addition to the paying agent, the Management Company must appoint an information agent in Germany to ensure that investors receive the information prescribed by the Investment Act in the German language (§131 sentence 2 InvG). This information comprises the latest annual and subsequent semi-annual report, the latest full and simplified sales prospectus, the fund's constitutive documents, and its issue and redemption prices. Any other documents and information which has to be published in the Home Member State, such as notices to unitholders, or to which the unitholders in the Home Member State are entitled, must be available in German and free of charge at the German information agent. As a unitholder is entitled to request this information from the information agent in printed form, it has to be ensured that the documentation is available in hard copy format or is readily available to be printed out (§121 para (1) sentence 5 InvG). Availability on the information agent's website is not sufficient.

The information agent does not need to be a German credit institution or German branch of a foreign credit institution. It can be and often is the same institution which acts as paying agent for the fund.

If the fund prospectuses or reports indicate that some or all of the above information may be obtained from another institution in Germany, the BaFin might question whether this entity has been appointed as an additional German information agent by the Management Company. For example, if the annual report states that prospectuses can be obtained from a German distributor who is not the same as the information agent appointed by the Management Company, the BaFin might still treat this distributor as an additional information agent. In these circumstances, an information agency confirmation (see chapter 4.3.4.1) from the relevant institution will be required and the specific information

---

[64] Vahldiek in Bödecker, see footnote 22, §131 A.

for German investors in the German full and simplified prospectus (see chapters 4.3.2.3.2 and 4.3.2.4.2) should name this institution as an additional information agent, otherwise the BaFin notification might be incomplete.

Although the Management Company is obliged to appoint a German information agent, the unitholders are not required to make use of such agent, but are free to request information directly from the Management Company.

4.2.3 Standardised services

The paying and information agents will enter into a contract with the Management Company. Some German credit institutions offer standardised paying and information agent services for foreign UCITS funds.

4.2.4 Termination

So long as a UCITS is registered with the BaFin for public marketing in Germany, the Management Company must ensure that at least one information agent and one paying agent for the fund in Germany are appointed. If a replacement agent is appointed there needs to be a seamless transition between the existing and the new agent. If the UCITS does not have a paying or information agent, the BaFin will prohibit further public marketing of the fund (see chapter 4.5.2.1). A new information or paying agent should be appointed before the existing contract ends in order to safeguard continuity if there is only one paying or information agent and its contract is terminated within the notice period. If the existing contract is terminated for cause without notice, the Management Company must appoint a new agent without undue delay. The Management Company must inform the BaFin about the change and file a confirmation from the new agent with the BaFin (see chapter 4.4.1).

4.2.5 Disclosure

The name and address of the paying and information agent and its statutory functions must be disclosed in the German versions of the full and simplified prospectus (§131 sentence 3 InvG) (see chapters 4.3.2.3.2 and 4.3.2.4.2).

4.3 Notification letter

The Management Company must submit a notification file to the BaFin which consists of the notification letter and the fund documentation. The content and form of the notification letter and the documents are set out in the BaFin Guidelines. A separate questionnaire needs to be filled out and separate documents attached for each fund notified to the BaFin, unless the funds are sub-funds under the same umbrella, in which case one questionnaire and one set of documents will be sufficient.

The Management Company should use the questionnaire included in the BaFin Guidelines for the notification letter: *Anzeige von EG Investmentanteilen zum öffentlichen Vertrieb in der Bundesrepublik Deutschland nach §132 des Investmentgesetzes (InvG)*. The Management Company has to print out, fill in and sign the questionnaire by its authorised representative or proxy. The questionnaire can be completed in German or English.[65] It should be addressed to[66]:

> Bundesanstalt für Finanzdienstleistungsaufsicht
> Lurgiallee 12
> 60439 Frankfurt.

The notification file comprising the letter and the attached documents has to be submitted to the BaFin in print by mail or courier. Submission by e-mail is not permitted.[67]

Part A of the questionnaire implements the CESR Guidelines. It covers the harmonised contents of the notification procedure according to Art. 46 and 6b para (5) of the UCITS Directive. Part B deals with information requirements which the Investment Act imposes outside the harmonised UCITS regime in relation to fund distribution, facilities for payments to be made to unitholders and for making compulsory information available to unitholders on the UCITS as referred to in Art. 44 and 45 of the UCITS Directive.

Individual items of information are to be listed under the appropriate numbers and headers of the questionnaire. If a number or header of the questionnaire is not applicable, it should

---

[65] BaFin Guidelines, V.
For subsequent communications with the BaFin, the Management Company should consult with the competent BaFin officer if English is acceptable, because the official language for administrative correspondence in Germany is German (see §23 para (1) VwVfG).
[66] BaFin Guidelines, VIII.d).
[67] BaFin Guidelines, IV.1).

still be included in the notification letter and marked "not applicable". In case of doubt a short explanation should be provided.

Documents not listed in the BaFin Guidelines as mandatory attachments to the notification letter should not be filed with the BaFin unless BaFin requests them. Consequently, subscription applications or advertisements of any kind should not be sent to the BaFin.

The following is an annotated translation of the mandatory notification letter.[68]

Notification of EU investment units for public distribution in the Federal Republic of Germany pursuant to §132 of the Investment Act

4.3.1 Part A: Harmonised part of the notification letter

4.3.1.1 Information about the fund

(1)   Name or trade name of the UCITS

The full name of the UCITS as stated in the prospectus and the UCITS certificate issued by the Home Member State Authority needs to be inserted here. For an umbrella fund, the full name of the umbrella fund should be inserted but not the names of the sub-funds.

(2)   Home Member State

(3)   Legal structure of the UCITS (please tick as applicable)

investment fund managed by a Management Company (contractual form)
unit trust
Investment Company (corporate form)

---

[68]   The translated questionnaire is highlighted in grey. Annotations and captions inserted for clarification purposes are without highlighting.

The first alternative applies to UCITS in contractual form, where unitholders have contractual but not corporate rights against the UCITS, for example a Luxembourg Fcp). The second alternative refers to UCITS set up as a common law trust. The third alternative applies to UCITS set up as corporate entities, where unitholders are corporate shareholders, for example a Luxembourg *société d'investissement à capital variable* (Sicav) or an Irish public limited company (plc). Whether or not the UCITS has outsourced its fund management to another Management Company is the object of heading 6, but is irrelevant under heading 3.

(4)   Does the UCITS have sub-funds (umbrella-fund)?

Yes   No

Name of fund and/or sub-fund(s) (please indicate if the fund is a standalone fund or a sub-fund)	Duration (if applicable)	WKN/ISIN (if available)

Please extend list, if necessary.

Name of fund/s: First, tick "yes" or "no" to indicate if the fund to be notified to the BaFin is a sub-fund of an umbrella fund. The sub-fund's name should be stated in full as it appears in the prospectus and the UCITS certificate of the Home Member State Authority. The umbrella fund's name should be stated only under heading 1 above. If the fund to be notified to the BaFin is a standalone fund, i.e. not a sub-fund under an umbrella fund, its full name which is already stated under heading 1 above, should be repeated here.

The BaFin's questionnaire does not adopt CESR's recommendation to name unit classes which are intended to be publicly marketed in Germany. This is because under the Investment Act the fund notification extends automatically to all existing and future unit classes regardless of whether they are intended for public distribution in Germany.

Duration: If the fund/s duration is limited in time, its termination date should be stated here.

WKN/ISIN:

WKN is the German securities identification number (*Wertpapierkennnummer*). WKNs can be applied for at www.wmdaten.de.

ISIN is the international securities identification number issued in the Home Member State. If the ISIN and, if applicable the WKN, are not available at the time of the BaFin filing the notification should not be incomplete. The numbers should, however, be filed with the BaFin as soon as they become available.

Although ISINs are the internationally recognised identification numbers for units, an additional application for WKNs is useful because a common request in Germany is to deal on the basis of the WKN and often IT systems still require the WKN.

4.3.1.2 Information about the Management Company

(6)   Management Company / self-managed Investment Company

Name or trade name, registered office, address (if not identical to registered office; for management companies which outsource their fund management this information is required for the outsourcing company and the appointed Management Company)

Name, telephone number, fax number and e-mail address of contact person

The BaFin requires that the contact person is located in the Home Member State of the the investment fund.

Duration of company (if applicable)

Scope of activities of Management Company in Host Member State

(7)   Possible additional commentaries of UCITS (as desired)

4.3.2 Required documentation

Attached documents (each in original fund language and German translation)

4.3.2.1 UCITS passport confirmation letter

(8) An original valid and up-to-date attestation granted by the Home Member State Authority that the provisions of Directive 85/611/EEC as amended from time to time have been complied with (the **UCITS passport**) or a copy of the original attestation self-certified by the Management Company's authorised directors or a third party empowered by written mandate that the copy is a true copy of the valid original in the company's possession and it is the latest version issued by the Home Member State Authority. The UCITS passport should be in the form set out in Annex I of the "CESR Guidelines to simplify the Notification Procedure of UCITS" (Ref CESR/06-120b).

The UCITS passport can be submitted with an English translation*; a German translation is not required.

*i.e. In the English original or with an English translation of the original language, for example, in French.

A key element of the notification to the BaFin is the fund's product passport, an up-to-date certificate from the Home Member State Authority stating that the fund complies with the provisions of the UCITS-Directive 85/611/EEC in the version of Amendment Directives 2001/107/EC and 2001/108/EC (UCITS III). The BaFin requires that the UCITS III certificate for the fund refers to the UCITS-Directive's passport for the fund and to the Management Company passport pursuant to the Amendment Directive 2001/107/EC.

In the Management Company passport, the Home Member State Authority attests that the Management Company complies with the UCITS III regulations for management companies or, if it does not, that it has appointed a UCITS III compliant Management Company to administer the fund. The model attestation in Annex I of the CESR Guidelines, which is set out below, combines the product passport with the Management Company passport.

If the Home Member State Authority issues an additional certificate, confirming which fund documents have most recently been brought to its attention, such certificate should also be filed with the BaFin.[69]

For an explanation of self-certification see chapter 4.3.3.1 below.

MODEL ATTESTATION TO MARKET UNITS OF UCITS IN AN EEA MEMBER STATE[70]

1 .... is the competent authority
(name of the competent Home Member State Authority)

2 in .... (the Home Member State)

3 address ....

4 telephone number ....

5 fax number...................................

6 e-mail address..................................

7 which carries out the duties provided for in Directive 85/611/EEC on the coordination of laws, regulations and administrative provisions relating to undertakings for collective investment in transferable securities (UCITS) (hereinafter, the Directive), as required by Art. 49 para (1) of the Directive.

8 For the purpose of Art. 46 para (1) and Art. 6b para (5) of the Directive, ...
(the competent Home Member State Authority)

9 certifies that: ....,
(the name of the UCITS, i.e. the name of the common fund/unit trust/Investment Company)

---

[69] The Irish Financial Regulator takes this approach.

[70] See Annex I to CESR Guidelines.

10 - has been set up on ....,
(date of approval of the fund rules of the UCITS)

11 - has registry no. ....,
(UCITS registry no. in the Home Member State, if any)

name of the authority......................................,
(name of the authority by which the register is conducted, if applicable)

12 - is based in ....,
(the Home Member State and details of the address of the UCITS head
office)

13 - is   a common fund/unit trust,

List of all sub-funds approved in the Home Member State, if applicable	
Serial no.	Name
1	
2	
3	
...	

• managed by the Management Company

....
(name of the Management Company)

14   an Investment Company,

List of all sub-funds approved in the Home Member State, if applicable	
Serial no.	Name
1	
2	
3	
...	

- that has designated as its Management Company

....
(name of the designated Management Company)

- that is self-managed

15   - is   a grandfathered UCITS I, i.e. it is fully compliant with the requirements of Directive 85/611/EEC prior to being amended by the Directive 2001/108/EC

16   - is   a UCITS III, i.e. it is fully compliant with the requirements of Directive 85/611/EEC as amended by Directive 2001/108/EC

17 .... also certifies that:
    (the Home Member State Authority)

18   a) ....
(name of the UCITS' Management Company, if applicable, according to what has been indicated above)

19 - is   a grandfathered UCITS I Management Company, i.e. it is fully compliant with the requirements of Directive 85/611/EEC prior to being amended by Directive 2001/107/EC

20 - is   a UCITS III Management Company, i.e. it is fully compliant with the requirements of Directive 85/611/EEC as amended by Directive 2001/107/EC

21   b) the latest version of the fund rules/instruments of incorporation has been approved by the competent Home Member State Authority on .... (date of approval);

22   Date ....

.... (signature of the representative of the Home Member State Authority)

.... (name in full and position of the undersigned representative of the Home Member State Authority)

4.3.2.2 Constitutive documents

(9) The **fund rules** of the investment fund or the **instruments of incorporation** of the investment company as approved by the Home Member State Authority. They need not be submitted separately if they are included as an integral part of the full prospectus.

(Please tick as appropriate)

     fund rules/instruments of incorporation are included in the full prospectus
     fund rules/instruments of incorporation are submitted separately

The Management Company must submit the latest constitutive documents of the fund, i.e. the management regulations, memorandum and articles of association or statutes, in the original language with a German translation. If the original language version does not show the original visa stamp of the Home Member State Authority, it must be self-certified (see chapter 4.3.3.1) as the most up-to-date version approved by or filed with the Home Member State Authority.

The constitutive documents form an integral part of the full prospectus and must be annexed thereto. As an integral part, the constitutive documents should be listed in the index of contents of the full prospectus and, if the prospectus is printed in hard copy format, not attached loosely but firmly bound in.

However, the constitutive documents need not be annexed to the full prospectus, provided that the unitholder is informed where in Germany the documents are available (German information agent; §§121 para (1) sentence 4, 131 sentence 2 InvG).

4.3.2.3 Full and simplified prospectus

(10) The **full and simplified prospectus** valid at the time of notification.

4.3.2.3.1 Number of copies

The notification file must contain the latest up-to-date full prospectus with all its addenda and supplements, if any, and the simplified prospectus of the fund.

Under the UCITS-Directive, the simplified and the full prospectus must include information necessary for investors to make an informed judgment of the proposed investment and of its risks.[71] The full prospectus must include a clear and easily understandable explanation of the fund's risk profile and at least the information provided for in Schedule A, Annex I to the UCITS Directive to the extent that such information does not already appear in the fund rules or constitutive documents annexed to the full prospectus.[72]

According to the UCITS Directive, the simplified prospectus must contain in summary form the key information provided for in Schedule C, Annex I to the UCITS Directive.[73] It must be structured and written in such a way that it can be easily understood by the average investor. Member States may permit the simplified prospectus to be attached as a removable part of the full prospectus. The simplified prospectus can be used as a marketing tool in all Member States without alteration except translation. Consequently, according to the UCITS Directive, Member States may not require further documents or additional information. The full and the simplified prospectus may be incorporated in a written document or in any durable medium which has an equivalent legal status as approved by the competent authorities.[74]

Each document must be submitted in the original fund language and show the original visa stamp of the Home Member State Authority or self-certification by the Management Company (see chapter 4.3.3.1).

The full prospectus, its addenda or supplements and the simplified prospectus in the original language of the fund, should each be accompanied by one German translation (see chapter 4.3.3.2).

---

[71] Article 28 para (1) UCITS Directive.
[72] Article 28 para (2) UCITS Directive.
[73] Article 28 para (3) UCITS Directive.
[74] Article 28 para (4) UCITS Directive.

4.3.2.3.2 Additional information for German investors

The BaFin routinely checks if the additional information for German investors as prescribed by the Investment Act (§131 sentence 3 InvG) and the BaFin Guidelines is properly included into the German version of the full and the simplified prospectus.

Location in the prospectus

Additional information for German investors should be set out in a separate chapter or an annex of the German full and simplified prospectus entitled *"Additional Information for Investors in Germany"*. This chapter or annex should be an integral part of the German prospectus, listed in the index of contents and included in the document's pagination. If the prospectus is printed, the chapter or annex needs to be a part of all hard copies, not attached loosely.

Since the additional information for German investors does not under German law need to be included in the original language version of the full or simplified prospectus, the original language version as approved by the Home Member State Authority and the German language version are allowed to be different in this respect. All information for German investors should be regularly updated. Its inclusion in the original language version would require every update to be filed with the Home Member State Authority. Prospectus management can be made more efficient if the additional information for German investors is not part of the original language version but only included in the German versions of the full and simplified prospectus.[75]

As well as setting out additional information for German investors in a separate chapter or annex, the BaFin also permits such information for German investors to be placed in the German prospectus in the context of the relevant subject matter, for example availability of documents or issue and redemption of units, provided that the same information is included in the same places in the original language prospectus. In this way the original and German language versions may be identical. On the other hand, it may be argued that distributing

---

[75] The Irish Financial Regulator takes the position that the additional information for German investors should be filed with it and therefore must be included in the English language prospectus. The BaFin and the Irish Financial Regulator have agreed that if the Management Company does not wish to include information for German investors in the English language prospectus, such information should still be included in a separate English language supplement for German investors. This supplement should be filed with the Irish Financial Regulator. A self-certified copy is then filed with the BaFin with a German translation which is an integral part of the German prospectus, whereas its English language counterpart remains separate from the English language prospectus. Having a separate English language document is meant to facilitate the filing procedure with the Irish Financial Regulator whenever updates to the information for German investors are necessary.

the information in this way makes it more difficult for the BaFin or the investor to find the additional information for German investors, and more laborious for the Management Company to keep it up-to-date.

If Home Member State law provides that the full and the simplified prospectus constitute a single document, the additional information for German investors needs to be included only once in the consolidated document, provided that the consolidated document is not subdivided into single parts in the course of distribution (see no. 4 BaFin FAQs).

Contents

The additional information for German investors should include the following (for umbrella funds see chapter 4.3.3.3):[76]

- corporate name and address of the paying agent(s) in Germany (see chapter 4.2.1);

- information that applications to redeem units and, in the case of umbrella funds applications to convert units (permitted for public distribution in Germany, if some but not all sub-funds under the same umbrella are permitted for public marketing in Germany) can be submitted to the paying agent in Germany;

- information that all fund payments to unitholders (redemptions proceeds, distributions and other payments) may be directed through the paying agent in Germany;

- name or corporate name and address of the information agent(s) in Germany (see chapter 4.2.2);

---

[76] In addition to the regulatory information requirements of the Investment Act, it is possible to add information on taxation in Germany in order to inform investors about the tax treatment of their fund units. Neither the insertion nor the omission of tax information will be criticized by the BaFin and the omission will not make the fund notification incomplete. From the prospectus liability view, however, prospectus information about taxation resembles a Gordian knot. If information of negative tax treatment which the average investor need not expect is not revealed in the prospectus this omission might give rise to investor claims for prospectus liability against the Management Company. If on the other hand tax information is included in the prospectus and is not updated, for example as a result of legal changes, the outdated information might lead to prospectus liability claims. For this reason it seems to be prudent to restrict prospectus information about taxation in Germany to the quintessential.

- information that the full and simplified prospectus with addenda and supplements (if any), the constitutive documents, if not an integral part of the full prospectus, the latest annual and subsequent semi-annual and quarterly reports (if any) of the investment fund are available in print and free of charge at the German information agent; that selling and redemption prices, and for umbrella funds conversion prices, are available free of charge at the German information agent. The information agent should have printed documents available in storage or should be able to print out documents at short notice because §121 para (1) sentence 3 InvG grants investors a right to obtain these documents in paper form (see chapter 6.1). It is also permitted to supply this information to investors by permanent data carrier (diskettes, CD-ROMs, DVDs) and these should be mentioned here if the information may be made available in this way.

If the full or simplified prospectus has addenda or supplements which are separate documents, not listed in the index of contents and, if the prospectus is printed in hard copy, not bound in but only loosely attached, these addenda or supplements need to be clearly identified with their date and/or number in the additional information for German investors. A general reference to all existing addenda and supplements is insufficient. This requirement is considered necessary to protect German investors who might otherwise not be aware of all existing addenda or supplements. Whenever a supplement or addendum is amended, removed from or added to the prospectus, the additional information for German investors needs to be updated.

Prospectuses frequently mention ancillary information, for example material contracts and legal statutes which are available to unitholders in the Home Member State. If information of this sort in included, the section for German investors should name these further documents and confirm their availability for inspection or collection by German investors free of charge at the German information agent. It should also be confirmed that such information is available in the same way as in the Home Member State. If copies can be obtained in the Home Member State, German investors should be able to obtain copies from the German information agent or, if documents can only be inspected in the Home Member State, inspection at the German information agent is sufficient.

- statement of the publication medium which is suitable for informing German investors in which issue and redemption prices and notices to unitholders are published (see chapter 4.4.2.2). The BaFin regards the following as suitable media: newspapers which are published in Germany, letters addressed to German investors[77], the *elektronischer Bundesanzeiger* and for issue and redemption prices also other electronic information media which are addressed to investors, such as the internet;

- a risk warning is required at the beginning of the prospectus for umbrella funds which distribute some but not all sub-funds to the German public (see chapter 4.3.3.3).

The following is an example of the information for German investors. Annotations are in *italics*.

"Additional information for investors in Germany

Unitholders can redeem their units in Germany through the German paying agent(s). The German paying agent(s) will pay the unitholder in cash or will transfer the redemption proceeds to the stated account of the unitholder. *In the case of umbrella funds*: Unitholders can also file applications for conversions with the German paying agent(s). Unitholders in Germany can receive all payments (such as redemptions and distributions) through the German paying agent(s).

German paying and information agent

The [investment Management Company] has appointed [full name and address] as paying and information agent in Germany.

Or, if paying and information agent are separate entities:
The [investment Management Company] has appointed [full name and address] as paying agent and [full name and address] as information agent in Germany.

If more than one paying agent and/or more than one information agent has been appointed:

---

[77] See no. 7 BaFin FAQs. This is an issue for units being held in nominee structures with the name and address of the final investor not being stated in the unitholder register.

Additional information/paying agent(s) is/are [full name(s) and address(es)].

The full prospectus [with its addenda/supplements No 1. dated [ ], no. 2 dated [ ], no. 3 dated [ ]], the simplified prospectus(es) [with its addenda/supplements No 1. dated [ ], no. 2 dated [ ], no. 3 dated [ ]], the fund rules/instruments of incorporation, the annual and sub-sequent semi-annual reports of the fund(s) are available in print and free of charge from the information agent(s). The issue and redemption [*and in the case of umbrella funds*: and conversion] prices of the fund units are also available free of charge from the information agent(s). [*Additional documents*] can be inspected [and copies obtained free of charge] from the German information agent(s).

Issue and redemption prices and notices to unitholders are published in the [*publication medium*]."

The disadvantage of additional national requirements is that simplified prospectuses of the same fund might not be consistent in different Member States. The fact that Host Member State Authorities require additional information defeats the concept of an easily understandable summary of material fund information. According to CESR's findings, the simplified prospectus is widely seen as having failed to achieve its objectives. In particular, there is considered to be a continuing lack of transparency about UCITS, especially their costs and risks; the information in the simplified prospectus is not easily understood and used by the average retail investor; the simplified prospectus itself is too lengthy and technical; it is costly and time-consuming to produce; its content often exceeds the Directive requirements; and does not assist comparisons between funds, particularly when cross-border sales are involved.[78]

UCITS IV will replace the simplified prospectus with "key investor information", a short format document containing in non-technical language only the essential elements relevant to the investment decision and presented in a way likely to be understood by retail investors. The key investor information will be harmonised to ensure adequate investor protection and comparability. The Host Member State Authority will no longer have the right to require additional information, and the key investor information must be used without alterations or supplements except for translation, in all Member States where the UCITS is notified to market its units. The intention is to use this core document unchanged

---

[78] CESR Press Release, July 2009, Ref.: CESR/09-678, "CESR moves forward its project to improve investor disclosures for UCITS".

across Europe, with the ultimate goals of maximising investor protection and improving the single market in UCITS.

UCITS IV sets out an exhaustive list of the type of information required in the key investor information, the details of which will be dealt with by the Commission in its implementation measures. The key investor information will constitute pre-contractual information. The essential elements will have to be kept up-to-date. Member States will have to ensure that a person will not incur civil liability solely on the basis of the key investor information including any translation, unless it is misleading, incorrect or inconsistent with the relevant parts of the prospectus. The key investor information will have to contain a clear warning in this respect. It will replace the simplified prospectus 12 months after the deadline for implementing the UCITS IV-Directive into national law, on 30 June 2011. The Member State Authorities will accordingly continue to accept simplified prospectuses until 30 June 2012.

4.3.2.4 Financial statements

(11) The latest published annual report and subsequent semi-annual report.

The Management Company must file the latest annual and subsequent semi-annual report with the BaFin. If in addition the fund publishes quarterly reports, the latest quarterly report following the latest annual or semi-annual report should also be filed. Reports must be submitted in the original fund language accompanied by a German translation.

Under the UCITS Directive, the accounting information in the annual report must be audited by one or more persons legally authorised to audit accounts in accordance with Council Directive 84/253/EEC[79].[80] The auditor's report including any qualifications, must be reproduced in full in the annual report. The auditors' report must be signed, but for the BaFin filing copies of the signed annual report are sufficient.

The annual report must include a balance sheet or statement of assets and liabilities, a detailed income and expenditure statement, a report on the activities during the financial

---

[79] Council Directive 84/253/EEC of 10 April 1984, based on Article 54 (3) (g) of the EEC Treaty on the approval of persons responsible for carrying out the statutory audits of accounting documents.
[80] Article 31 UCITS Directive.

year, information provided for in Schedule B, Annex I to the Directive, and any significant information to enable investors to make an informed judgment of the development of the activities of the UCITS and its results.[81] The semi-annual report must include at least the information provided for in chapters I to IV of Schedule B, Annex I to the Directive; where a UCITS has paid or proposes to pay an interim dividend, the figures must state the results after tax for the half year concerned and the interim dividend paid or proposed.[82]

4.3.2.4.1 Deadlines for filing reports

The notification for public marketing should be timed so that the filing deadlines for the next annual or semi-annual report do not fall within the notification period. Annual reports must be published and submitted to the BaFin at the latest four months following the end of the fund's accounting year and semi-annual reports two months following the end of the first half of the fund's accounting year.[83] If any such filing deadlines fall within the notification period, before the BaFin has confirmed the completeness of the notification without material objection to public distribution commencing, and if the relevant financial report is not filed with the BaFin in time, the BaFin might regard the notification as incomplete and the waiting period will not start running.

4.3.2.4.2 Additional information for German investors

Location in the report

Reports should contain additional information for German investors in a separate paragraph or chapter or included alongside similar information in the report. Such information should form an integral part of the report, not attached loosely but firmly bound in. It needs to be regularly updated. As stated above in relation to prospectuses, under German law this additional information only needs to be included in the German version of the report.

---

[81] Article 28 para (5) UCITS Directive.
[82] Article 28 para (6) UCITS Directive.
[83] Article 27 para (2) UCITS-Directive.

Reports should contain the following additional information for German investors:

- the German information agent's name and address and a statement that full and simplified prospectus(es) can be obtained from the information agent. This information requirement, although not expressly mentioned in the BaFin Guidelines, exists because reports are regarded as marketing material which under the Investment Act should inform investors about the prospectus being available at the German information agent(s). For example:

  > "The full and simplified prospectus(es) of the fund are available in print and free of charge from the German information agent: [name and address]";

- if a report states that other information or documents are available for investors in the Home Member State, it needs to add that they are available in the same way from the German information agent(s). The statements about the availability of information and documents should be identical in reports and the prospectuses (see chapter 4.3.2.3.2);

- if a report identifies publication media in which notices to unitholders are published in the Home Member State, it should state the name of the media in which unitholder notices are published in Germany. Such media should be the same as those stated in the full and simplified prospectus (see chapter 4.3.2.3.2);

- under the UCITS-Directive[84], annual and semi-annual reports should contain a complete list of changes to the securities portfolio during the reporting period, including the number of purchases and sales of securities. If this list is not included or is incomplete, the BaFin requires the report to state that a complete list of changes to the portfolio is available free of charge from the German information agent;

---

[84] Article 28 para (5) and (6) in connection with Annex I, Schedule B IV.

- umbrella funds which distribute some but not all sub-funds to the German public must have a risk warning at the beginning of each report (see chapter 4.3.3.3); and

- German reports should not contain any advertisement about the Management Company or its funds.

4.3.3 General

(12)   Notes:

The latest versions of the documents, as approved by or filed with the Home Member State Authority, must be attached to the notification letter and submitted to the BaFin. A certification by the Management Company's authorised directors or a third person who is empowered by written mandate to act on behalf of the Management Company, that the versions of the documents to be filed are the latest approved by or filed with the Home Member State Authority, will be accepted.

The notification letter may refer to documents which have already been sent to the BaFin if still valid. The UCITS passport (or its copy) must be sent to the BaFin in any case.

Single copies of all documents have to be filed in their most up-to-date version as prepared, filed with or approved by the Home Member State Authority. Whether the relevant document has to be approved or just filed with the Home Member State Authority will depend on the UCITS regulations as implemented in the Home Member State.

If sub-funds under an umbrella fund are notified to the BaFin for public marketing, documents which have already been filed for the prior notification of other sub-funds under the same umbrella do not need to be submitted again, unless the versions on file with the BaFin are no longer the most recent. This does not apply to the UCITS passport, which has to be renewed with each sub-fund notification.

4.3.3.1 Self-certification of documents

All documents should show the original visa stamp of the Home Member State Authority if available, or should be self-certified by the Management Company. Self-certification like the visa stamp should be upon the document itself. It can be in German or in English. If it is in another language it needs to be accompanied by a German translation.

The self-certification has to specify the name and function of its signatories. This may be done by printing their name and function beneath their signatures. If self-certification is not done by the executive body of the Management Company but by proxy, a list of authorised signatures should be submitted to the BaFin, including names, functions or titles and specimen signatures of proxies. The list should also state each proxy's authorisation on behalf of the Management Company, if a sole signatory is sufficient or if two (or more) signatories are required. Once the list has been filed with the BaFin, it will be relied upon by the BaFin for subsequent fund notifications, unless the Management Company changes or revokes the list. The list must be signed by the executive body of the Management Company, and the names and functions of the signatories set out in print.

4.3.3.2 Language and translations

The full and simplified prospectus, constitutive documents and reports must be submitted to the BaFin in their original language version as reviewed or issued by the Home Member State Authority, with a German translation. There are two exceptions from the translation requirement as follows:

> ➢ the UCITS certificate may be submitted in English ;

> ➢ umbrella funds which distribute only some sub-funds to the German public, are not required to translate into German information in prospectuses, constitutive documents or reports about sub-funds which are not publicly marketed and therefore not notified to the BaFin. The original fund language even in the German document versions is acceptable.

The German documents must be exact word for word translations of the original language versions. They should not omit anything, even if it is irrelevant for the German market. For example, if the original language prospectus includes specific information for other countries where the fund will be distributed, such information should be translated into German. Textual additions, changes or omissions or ordering the text differently from the original language version (as approved by or filed with the Home Member State Authority) are prohibited, unless permitted by the UCITS-Directive and German law. Specific information for German investors is a permitted addition (see chapters 4.3.2.3.2 and 4.3.2.4.2) and the above-mentioned exemption for umbrella funds is a permitted omission.

German terminology should be consistent throughout the German translation of the fund documentation. For example, only the Management Company which holds the UCITS III passport for management companies and manages the fund should be designated *"Verwaltungsgesellschaft"*. Other managers may be called *"Manager"*, and investment advisors may be called *"Anlageberater"*. Figures must be written in continental style (100.000,00), not US/UK style (100,000.00). Fund names should be stated correctly throughout the fund documentation, in the same way they are used by the Home Member State Authority in the UCITS certificate. Abbreviations are only permitted to the extent fund names are defined.

A correct German translation is crucial for the fund's notification with the BaFin and to prevent prospectus liability. Investors' claims against the Management Company are triggered if information contained in the full or simplified prospectus which is of material significance to evaluate fund units, is inaccurate or incomplete (see chapter 7.3.1). Inaccuracy or incompleteness can be caused by poor translation. The German prospectus versions are authoritative for claims of prospectus liability by German investors.

Official verifications of German translations are not required. German prospectuses may contain a disclaimer that their original language versions are authoritative, except in respect of investors' claims of prospectus liability (§123 sentences 3 and 4 InvG).

4.3.3.3 Partial registration of umbrella funds

The complete documentation in the original fund language (see chapter 4.3.2) relating to all umbrella fund sub-funds should be filed with the BaFin at the time of the first sub-fund notification. For all subsequent sub-fund notifications the Management Company should arrange with the BaFin that only those documents relating to the new sub-funds need to be submitted, such as simplified prospectuses, addenda or supplements to the full prospectus, and documents relating to already notified funds which have been amended since their last filing with the BaFin. Documents which are unchanged since their previous filing with the BaFin generally do not need to be submitted again, and the notification letter can state that the versions already on file with the BaFin are still the most current. This does not apply to the UCITS passport which has to be renewed with each sub-fund notification. In addition, the German paying and information agent confirmations should be resubmitted with an updated list of sub-funds (see chapter 4.3.4.1).

German documents, in particular prospectuses and reports, which contain only information on sub-funds which are not intended for public marketing in Germany, do not need to be submitted to the BaFin. Similarly, if constitutive documents, full or simplified prospectus(es) or reports which are filed with the BaFin contain information on such funds, this information can remain in the original fund language in the German versions of these documents. Sections which only refer to sub-funds which are not intended for public marketing in Germany do not need to be translated into German. However, the Management Company if it wishes to do so is free to prepare complete German document versions.

If the fund notification concerns some but not all sub-funds under an umbrella fund and if the umbrella contains sub-funds which are not notified to the BaFin, the Investment Act requires the German full and the simplified prospectus, the reports and constitutive documents, if they contain any information on the non-notified sub-funds, to exhibit a typographically highlighted notice in a prominent position that for these sub-funds no notification to the BaFin has been made und that they are not permitted for public marketing to investors in Germany (§131 sentence 3 InvG and BaFin Guidelines VII.). The warning notice needs to name precisely the sub-funds concerned.

Such as warning notice is necessary in every case where at least one of several but not all of the sub-funds under the same umbrella fund are permitted for public marketing in Germany. For investor protection, the notice must be designed and located in the prospectus to catch the investor's eye immediately. In the full and simplified prospectus the warning notice should be part of the section dealing with specific information for German investors and printed in bold typeface. In constitutive documents and reports the warning notice should follow the cover page and therefore must be printed on page two of the prospectus in bold typeface. Whenever a new sub-fund which is not notified to the BaFin is set up under the umbrella fund, the warning notice should be updated. The same applies whenever a sub-fund mentioned in the notice is subsequently notified to the BaFin or is renamed or closed and liquidated.

The warning notice should also be included in the original language version of a document which contains information about fund distribution in Germany, for example the name of German distributors, paying or information agent(s) or reference to the fund being permitted for public marketing in Germany or relating to its notification to the BaFin.

If, contrary to CESR's recommendations (Guideline 10 no. 3 of the CESR Guidelines), a separate full prospectus has been approved by the Home Member State Authority for each sub-fund rather than one full prospectus for all sub-funds, the Management Company's authorised directors or a third person empowered by written mandate to act on behalf of the Management Company must self-certify that the specific information for German investors is the same in each German full prospectus or otherwise indicate where the differences lie. The same applies for annual and semi-annual reports, if they are separate for each sub-fund.

4.3.3.4 Power of Attorney

A professional agent may act as proxy for the Management Company in its dealings with the BaFin, but this is not required by law. If the notification is made by proxy, for instance by a German law firm and not by the executive body of the Management Company, a duly signed power of attorney should be included into the notification file. The power of attorney must specify the name and function of at least one natural person as proxy.

The power of attorney must entitle the proxy to file the notification with the BaFin in the name of the Management Company and to make and receive all declarations necessary for the filing. It should also state the extent to which the proxy is authorised to certify on behalf of the Management Company, in particular that a document submitted to the BaFin is a true copy of the most up-to-date original as approved by the Home Member State Authority.

It may also be expedient to authorise the proxy to supplement, extend and withdraw the notification, and represent the Management Company to the BaFin after the fund has been permitted to market publicly in Germany. The proxy needs to be able to respond to BaFin recommendations on the filing within whatever timelines are suggested. Representation on a sustained basis is also relevant, because once the fund is marketed in Germany it has to comply with ongoing regulatory duties, observance of which is monitored by the BaFin (see chapter 4.4). If the BaFin has a contact person who can easily be reached by phone and speaks German, the relationship between the fund and the BaFin is likely to be facilitated. This person does not have to be a German resident.

The power of attorney may be extended to all existing and future sub-funds of umbrella funds. There will then be no need to file another power of attorney if at a later stage additional sub-funds are notified for public marketing with the BaFin.

If the proxy also represents the Management Company to a stock exchange, the powers of attorney for the BaFin and the stock exchange can be combined in a single document.

The power of attorney must be signed by the Management Company's authorised directors whose names and functions are stated. Their name and function can be printed beneath their signature. The power of attorney must be in the German language. In practice, it is often in German and the fund language with the German version being authoritative.

4.3.4 PART B: Non-harmonised part of the notification letter

Information and documents required for the notification under German Law

4.3.4.1 Confirmations of paying and information agent

(13) Conditions for public distribution in Germany
(see the respective notes in the BaFin Guidelines)

(13.1) Additional documents to be filed:

(13.1.1) Confirmation pursuant to §131 sentence 1 InvG, paying agent

See (13.1.2).

(13.1.2) Confirmation pursuant to §131 sentence 1 InvG, information agent

As part of its notification file, the Management Company should submit an up-to-date letter from a German credit institution or the German branch of a credit institution with its registered seat abroad (see chapter 4.2.1) confirming that it has assumed the role of paying agent. In addition, an up-to-date letter from an agent in Germany should be submitted which confirms that it has assumed the role of information agent for the fund in Germany (see chapter 4.2.2).

Pursuant to the BaFin Guidelines, the paying agent's confirmation should be worded as follows:

> "We hereby confirm that we have assumed for . . . [name of investment fund/Investment Company/name of sub-fund of umbrella fund[85]] the function of a paying agent within the meaning of §131 sentence 1 InvG. We shall forward designated payments to the investors and shall process the redemption of units (in the case of umbrella funds the conversion as well) by the Investment Company as soon as the respective redemption applications (in the case of

---

[85] Pursuant to §132 and §2 para (11) sentence 2 no. 4 InvG the paying and information agent confirmation must only refer to the notified sub-funds in case of partial sub-fund notifications.

umbrella funds also the conversion applications) have been submitted." (for a German translation see BaFin Guidelines III.)

Pursuant to the BaFin Guidelines, the information agent's confirmation should be worded as follows:

> "We hereby confirm that we have assumed for . . . [name of investment fund/Investment Company/name of sub-fund of umbrella fund[86]] the function of an information agent within the meaning of §131 sentence 2 InvG and accordingly we will keep available the required information for investors." (for a German translation see BaFin Guidelines III.)

If one entity has been appointed as paying agent and information agent, the wording of the above confirmations should be consolidated as follows:

> "We hereby confirm that we have assumed for . . . [name of investment fund/Investment Company/name of sub-fund of umbrella fund[87]] the function of a paying and information agent within the meaning of §131 InvG. We shall forward designated payments to the investors and shall process the redemption of units (in the case of umbrella funds also the conversion) by the Investment Company as soon as the respective redemption applications (in the case of umbrella funds also the conversion applications) have been submitted. Furthermore, we will keep available the required information for investors." (for a German translation see BaFin Guidelines III.).

The paying agent's and information agent's confirmation should be addressed to the BaFin and signed by the agent's authorised representative(s). The confirmations should be submitted to the BaFin as signed originals. The BaFin will also accept certified copies of the originals, provided that the Management Company's authorised directors or a third person who is empowered by written mandate to act on behalf of the Management Company, certifies that the respective copy is a true copy of a valid original which is in the possession of the Management Company. The paying and information agent certificate(s) should be submitted to the BaFin only in the German language.

---

[86] See footnote 85.

[87] See footnote 85.

4.3.4.2 Notification fee

(13.1.3)   Proof of payment of the notification fee (§132 para 2 no. 6 InvG)

The BaFin's fee for processing the fund notification is EUR 1,500 per (sub-)fund. It has to be paid before the notification is filed with the BaFin. The total fee for all (sub-)funds to which the notification relates should be forwarded to the following account:

> Bundeskasse Trier (payee)
> Deutsche Bundesbank, Filiale Saarbrücken
> BLZ 590 000 00
> Account-no. 590 010 20
> IBAN: DE 81590000000059001020
> BIC: MARKDEF 1590

with the following identification:

> "BaFin, ... (name of fund(s), to which the notification refers), AnzGeb."

The name of the (sub-)fund(s) needs to be printed in full, unless precluded by technical constraints, such as a limited number of digits on the remittance slip. The fee must be credited to the above account in full and it should not be reduced by bank charges or other costs.

A copy of the remittance slip has to be filed with the BaFin as proof of payment, otherwise the notification file is not regarded as complete and the two months waiting period will not start running.

4.3.4.3 Ways and means of envisaged distribution in Germany

(13.2) Information about the arrangements for public distribution and the type and manner of distribution in Germany.

(13.2.1)   Paying agent

Please state corporate name, legal form, registered office and address of the paying agent and that payments designated for investors are made and redemptions and, if applicable, conversions of units are processed through the paying agent.

Please state name or corporate name and address of the information agent(s) in Germany where and how the sales documentation (full and simplified sales prospectus, annual and subsequent semi-annual report, the fund rules or instrument of incorporation) and the other required information and documents (issue and redemption prices and any other document and information, which has to be published in the Home Member State and/or to which the unitholders in the Home Member State are entitled) are available for investors free of charge. Please also provide a description of the ways and means of their publication (publication media, for example newspapers published in Germany, letters to unitholders in Germany[88], electronic edition of the German Federal Gazette; in relation to issue and redemption prices also electronic information media addressed to German unitholders)

(13.2.3)   Information about distribution and distributors

(this list should be extended, if necessary)

The ways and means of the designated marketing of units in Germany should be explained here, for example if it is to be through German branches, independent external financial agents or credit institutions. All distributors have to be properly licensed (see chapter 5). Please state the name or corporate name, legal form, registered office and address of all German resident distributors, which are authorised by the Management Company to sell fund units in Germany. If there is a complex distribution network it may be worthwhile to agree with the BaFin that only the main German distributors need be mentioned here.

4.3.4.4 Additional confirmation requirements

(14.)   Confirmation by the UCITS

I hereby confirm that the documents attached to this notification letter contain all relevant information provided for in Directive 85/611/EEC (UCITS-Directive) and CESR's guidelines to simplify the notification procedure of UCITS (Ref: CESR/06-120b) and the German provisions for the notification procedure pursuant to §132 Investment Act. Documents in foreign languages are submitted together with a German translation. The German translations are diligent translations of the original documents submitted to or approved by the Home Member State Authority and do not contain any textual additions,

---

[88]   Provided that all unitholders can be reached by letter, because their addresses are known.

changes, omissions or different text order. These have only been made in the German versions to the extent decreed by UCITS-Directive (Art. 44(1) and Art. 45 of the Directive (in particular Schedule A, Annex I, no. 4 of the Directive for full prospectus) in its current edition and applicable German law rules.

_____

Date and place   (signature of the authorised signatory of the foreign Management Company or of a third person authorised by written mandate to act on behalf of the notifying Management Company)

_____

(name in full and position of the undersigned authorised signatory(ies) of the Management Company or of the third person authorised by written mandate to act on behalf of the notifying Management Company)

4.4 Reporting, information and fee requirements subsequent to UCITS notification

Once the units of a UCITS are admitted to public distribution in Germany and after the two months notification period has expired without the BaFin prohibiting public marketing, the Management Company has to observe ongoing regulatory reporting and information requirements in order to maintain the fund's public distribution status.

4.4.1 Updating the BaFin

4.4.1.1 General

The Management Company of each fund notified to the BaFin is obliged to update the BaFin periodically with the latest fund reports, prospectuses and constitutive documents (§122 para (1) sentence 3 InvG). In addition, any publications which the Management Company has to make in its Home Member State and in Germany also need to be filed with the BaFin.

The formal requirements for filing updated documents, reports and their German translations with the BaFin after the original fund notification are the same as those applying to the original BaFin filing (see chapters 4.3.2 and 4.3.3). The documents and publications must be in the German language or accompanied by a German translation (§123 InvG).

When documents are updated, the information for German investors in the full and simplified prospectus often needs to be modified, especially if the updates relate to prospectus supplements or addenda. Whenever prospectuses or constitutive documents are updated and reports are finalised, the Management Company should ensure that any previous comments to it by the BaFin about information for German investors have been dealt with, because this will be checked by the BaFin.

The Management Company should make serious efforts to comply with applicable time limits (see chapters 4.4.1.2 and 4.4.1.3). If deadlines cannot be kept, the Management Company should agree with the BaFin before they expire as to extensions. The BaFin has discretionary power to prohibit public marketing of a fund (see chapter 4.5.2.2), if updates are not submitted properly with their German translations and in due time.

Under UCITS IV, the Home Member State Authority has to ensure that the BaFin has electronic access to document updates and if required, their translations. The UCITS will only have to notify the BaFin of amendments and state where the fund documentation (constitutive documents, prospectus, latest annual report and any subsequent semi-annual report, key investor information and if required, their translations) can be obtained electronically. If arrangements for marketing which are outlined in the notification letter change (see chapter 4.3.4.3), or there is a change in the share classes to be marketed in Germany, the UCITS must give written notice to the BaFin before it implements the relevant change.[89]

4.4.1.2 Financial statements

The Management Company must send the annual and semi-annual reports to the Home Member State Authority and file them with the BaFin in their original language together with a German translation within four months of the end of the fiscal year[90] and within two months of the end of the half year[91].

4.4.1.3 Amendments to fund documentation

Under the UCITS Directive, the Management Company is obliged to keep the essential elements of the simplified and the full prospectus up-to-date[92]. The Management Company

---

[89] Article 93 para (8) UCITS IV Directive.
[90] Articles 27 para (2) and 32 UCITS Directive.
[91] Article 27 para (2) UCITS Directive.
[92] Article 30 UCITS Directive.

must send the prospectuses and any amendments thereto, as well as annual and semi-annual reports, to the Home Member State Authority.[93] The replacement of the Management Company or the depositary and changes to the constitutive documents (fund rules or instruments of incorporation) require the approval of the Home Member State Authority.[94]

The Management Company is not obliged to inform the BaFin about any changes before they take effect or before they are published in the Home Member State. After they are first used in the Home Member State, the Management Company has to submit to the BaFin without undue delay the full and simplified prospectus (with supplements or addenda, if any) and constitutive documents which have been updated or modified, with an updated German translation. Each amendment to a document on file with the BaFin requires a resubmission, even if the change is only to a name or address.

After the Management Company has notified the BaFin of changes and has submitted the relevant updates, there is no waiting period for disseminating the new documentation in Germany.

The Management Company should set out in a letter to the BaFin the changes to the last version of the document filed with the BaFin. When reviewing updated documents, the BaFin is generally not bound to complete its review within any particular time. The BaFin may request that the information for German investors is modified in an update. The BaFin will not contact the Management Company or its representative unless it requests changes to such information. If the Management Company is planning to print new documents, it would be prudent to contact the BaFin officer in charge after a reasonable period to ask for comments or oral approval. If the quantity of updated German documentation is substantial, but the Management Company would still prefer to obtain the BaFin's oral approval soon after filing the documents, the Management Company should give the BaFin advance notice and discuss if the BaFin has capacity to review the documentation within the Management Company's timetable.

If changes are made to fund documents which have been filed with the BaFin while the original notification for public marketing is pending, the two months waiting period might be extended because the BaFin will need additional time to complete its review (see chapter 4.1.4).

---

[93]   Article 32 UCITS Directive.
[94]   Article 4 para (4) UCITS Directive.

4.4.1.4 Publications

Publications the Management Company has to make in its Home Member State and in Germany should be filed with the BaFin without undue delay. The BaFin is interested in receiving copies of any newspaper or other publications to unitholders which show the medium through which the information is disseminated and the publication date. Copies of publications relating to changes in the fund should be accompanied by the corresponding amended fund documentation for the BaFin's easier reference.

4.4.2 Informing investors

4.4.2.1 General

The Management Company must keep investors informed about the fund by distributing the fund's full and simplified prospectus, constitutive documents, annual and subsequent semi-annual reports in the Host Member State in accordance with the procedures of the Home Member State.[95] These documents must be provided in the official language(s) of the Host Member State or one of them if more than one, or in a language approved by the competent authority of the Host Member State.

Consequently, the Management Company is obliged to publish information and documentation in Germany and to provide the German information agent in a timely manner with the current fund documentation and any updates, each in the German language (§122 para (1) sentence 1 InvG). The provisions of the Home Member State apply accordingly to the scope, contents and timing of the publication (§122 para (1) sentence 2 InvG). Failure to comply with these duties may lead to the fund being prohibited from public marketing in Germany (see chapter 4.5.2.2).

These obligations will continue under UCITS IV. The Management Company will have to provide the same information and documents including amendments, to investors in a Host Member State as it is required to provide to investors in its Home Member State. Such information or documents will have to be made available as prescribed by the laws, regulations or administrative provisions of the Host Member State.

---

[95] Article 47 UCITS Directive.

4.4.2.2 Publications

4.4.2.2.1 Issue and redemption prices

The Management Company must regularly publish issue and redemption prices of the fund units in Germany. The publication in Germany should track in its frequency the publication in the Home Member State. Whenever publication of issue and redemption prices occurs in the Home Member State, it should take place in Germany at the same time. Under the UCITS Directive, these publications occur each time the UCITS issues or repurchases units, and at least twice a month.[96] The Home Member State Authority may, however, permit a UCITS to reduce the frequency to once a month on condition that such derogation does not prejudice the interests of the unitholders.

The Management Company is free to choose a suitable information medium to publish issue and redemption prices, provided that it comes within the BaFin Guidelines. The BaFin currently regards as suitable:

- nationwide newspapers with their place of publication in Germany;

- letters addressed to German investors, provided that every investor in Germany can be reached by letter;[97]

- the elektronischer Bundesanzeiger; and

- other electronic information media addressed to investors in Germany.

4.4.2.2.2 Unitholder notices

Documents or information which the Management Company is obliged to publish in the Home Member State (other than prospectuses, constitutive documents or reports, which must be available for German investors at the German information agent, see chapter 4.2.2) must be published in Germany at the same time as in the Home Member State. Publication required to be made more than once in the Home Member State must happen in Germany the same number of times.

---

[96] Article 34 UCITS Directive.

[97] See footnote 88.

Publication in Germany should be a literal translation of the publication in the original language. Unless the BaFin expressly agrees otherwise, summaries or omissions are not permitted.

The Management Company may choose a suitable information medium. For general information to unitholders, the BaFin considers that the same media are appropriate as for issue and redemption prices (see chapter 4.4.2.2.1), except for electronic information media other than the electronic edition of the German Federal Gazette. The choice of publication media must be stated in the information for German investors in the prospectuses (see chapter 4.3.2.3.2) to enable investors to monitor it.

Lengthy information notices, such as extensive newspaper publications, can be expensive. In advance of the publication date the Management Company might want to discuss with the BaFin what is appropriate information for unitholders. One approach would be publication of abbreviated versions of the notices in addition to making more extensive information available at the German information agent. If this approach is taken the name and address of the German information agent and the availability of the full version from the agent should be stated in the publication.

If the original language of a publication refers to information or documents being available for investors in the Home Member State, the publication in Germany needs to state that the same information or document is available for German investors from the German information agent, whose name and address should be set out in the publication.

4.4.2.3 Information agent

The Management Company should supply the German information agent with the latest German language versions of its annual and subsequent semi-annual reports, full and simplified prospectus including supplements or addenda, and constitutive documents if not already included in the full prospectus, each as filed with the BaFin (see chapter 4.1), and also with the latest issue, redemption and, in the case of umbrella funds, conversion prices. Hard copies of the documents should be available from the information agent. As German investors are by law entitled to receive printed copies of fund documentation, the information agent should be provided with printed copies of all relevant documents or be prepared to print out such documents if requested by a unitholder or interested party (§121 para (1) sentence 5 InvG).

The information agent should be supplied with the most recent fund documentation, subject to the same time limits which apply to the relevant BaFin filing. Audited annual reports should be provided to the German information agent within four months following the end of the Management Company's fiscal year and semi-annual reports within two months following the end of the the Management Company's fiscal half year. Prospectuses and constitutive documents should be provided to the German information agent without undue delay after they are first published in the Home Member State.

The German information agent must be supplied with additional documentation or information in German which unitholders are entitled to receive or inspect in the Home Member State and ensure such information is available for investors (see chapter 4.3.2.3.2). This will include material contracts and other information specified in the information for German investors in the prospectuses. If investors in the Home Member State can obtain printed copies, German investors must also be able to obtain printed German copies from the German information agent. If investors in the Home Member State are only entitled to inspect documents but not to make copies the same should apply to German investors at the German information agent.

4.4.3 Annual fees subsequent to notification

For each (sub-)fund registered for public marketing in Germany, the Management Company must pay an annual regulatory fee of EUR 500 to the BaFin.[98] The amount is due at the beginning of each calendar year starting from the calendar year following the year in which the fund was notified for public distribution to the BaFin. The Management Company has to pay the fee for the correct number of funds and sub-funds currently registered at the end of a calendar year, and for sub-funds which were closed down and duly deregistered with the BaFin before the end of the previous year. The BaFin will send a reminder if the fee is not paid promptly. If despite BaFin's reminder the fee is not paid, the BaFin may prohibit public marketing of the fund (§133 para (4) InvG).

---

[98] *Anhang zur FinDAGKostV (in der ab 31.10.2009 gültigen Fassung) no. 4.1.3.2.*
http://www.bafin.de/cln_171/SharedDocs/Downloads/DE/Service/Aufsichtsrecht/findagkostv__ab__091031__anl,templateId=raw,property=publicationFile.doc/findagkostv_ab_091031_anl.doc

4.5 Termination of public distribution of UCITS

4.5.1 Termination by the Investment Management Company

4.5.1.1 Investment funds which continue to exist in the Home Member State

4.5.1.1.1 Notification to the BaFin

The Management Company at any time can waive the distribution rights for a fund which is still registered in the Home Member State, if it decides to stop public marketing and distribution of the fund units in the Home Member State and Germany, or only in Germany. This is done by sending a letter to the BaFin declaring the Management Company's intention to waive distribution rights in Germany with immediate effect or by reference to a specified future date.

4.5.1.1.2 Umbrella funds

If the Management Company intends to stop public distribution of some but not of all of the sub-funds of an umbrella fund, it must update the fund documentation in order to include warning notices on prospectuses, constitutive documents and reports about the limited distribution of sub-funds in Germany (see chapter 4.3.3.3) and obtain a new confirmation from the German paying and information agent (see chapter 4.3.4.1) (§133 para (9) sentence 1 InvG). Before the updated documents can be made available to investors they must be filed with the BaFin together with a new confirmation by the German paying and information agent (§133 para (9) sentence 2 InvG).

A fee of EUR 750 per sub-fund for deregistration has to be paid to the BaFin[99] for it to handle the updated documentation. The fee should be paid into the account mentioned in chapter 4.3.4.2 with the following identification:

"BaFin, ... (name of fund to which the notification refers), DeRegGeb."[100]

The name of the sub-fund should be printed in full, unless precluded by technical constraints, such as limited space on the remittance slip. The fee must be credited to the

---

[99] *Anhang zur FinDAGKostV (in der ab 31.10.2009 gültigen Fassung) no. 4.1.3.6.*
http://www.bafin.de/cln_171/SharedDocs/Downloads/DE/Service/Aufsichtsrecht/findagkostv__ab__09 1031__anl,templateId=raw,property=publicationFile.doc/findagkostv_ab_091031_anl.doc
[100] See BaFin Guidelines VI.

BaFin's account in full and not reduced by bank charges or other costs. As proof of payment a copy of the remittance slip should be filed with the BaFin.

If distribution of the whole umbrella fund in Germany is terminated, only chapter 4.5.1.1.1 applies.

4.5.1.1.3 Informing investors

The Management Company must inform German investors by publishing a notice of the cessation of public distribution in Germany in the electronic edition of the German Federal Gazette[101] without undue delay and must send the BaFin proof of the publication (§133 para (8) sentence 1 and para (9) sentence 3 InvG). If the Management Company fails to publish a notice, after one reminder the BaFin is entitled to make the publication itself at the expense of the Management Company (§133 para (8) sentence 2 and para (9) sentence 4 InvG).

If the fund has German investors, the Management Company can waive distribution rights in Germany, but should consider whether interests of investors, such as their current tax status, need to be safeguarded. Publication of tax transparency data is not regarded as public marketing in Germany (see chapter 3.1.2.2.5) and is permitted after the fund has lost its authorisation for public marketing.

4.5.1.2 Investment funds which cease to exist in the Home Member State

4.5.1.2.1 Notification to the BaFin

Liquidation

The Management Company is obliged to inform the BaFin if a sub-fund or fund is closed and wound-up in the Home Member State. The Management Company must inform the BaFin in writing of the closure and waive distribution rights for the sub-fund or fund in Germany. The waiver filed with the BaFin should enclose a copy of the Home Member State Authority's approval of the fund's deregistration, preferably self-certified, with a German translation if applicable.

---

[101] http://www.ebundesanzeiger.de

Often a fund closure is due to a fund merger. Each fund merger should be notified to BaFin and the merged fund should be deregistered with the BaFin. If the surviving fund changes its name, or if its prospectuses or constitutive documents are updated, as frequently occurs upon a merger, such change needs to be notified to the BaFin and documentation updates should be submitted to the BaFin (see chapter 4.4.1.3). The updates should also be deposited with the German information agent (see chapter 4.4.2.3). The BaFin requires a copy of the Home Member State Authority's written approval to the merger, preferably self-certified, with a German translation. The BaFin filing and the deposit with the German information agent should take place without undue delay once the Home Member State Authority has approved the merger and the new fund documentation.

4.5.1.2.2 Informing investors

The publication duties mentioned in chapter 4.5.1.1.3 above do not arise if the fund ceases to exist as a result of a liquidation or merger in the Home Member State. The same applies to the duty to include or update warning notices for German investors in chapter 4.5.1.1.2 above, where only some but not all sub-funds under an umbrella fund are publicly distributed in Germany. If the sub-fund which is permitted for public distribution in Germany ceases to exist in the Home Member State, only general investor information duties apply, whereby German investors might need to be informed beforehand or invited to a shareholder meeting, depending on how shareholders in the Home Member State are informed (§122 para (1) InvG) (see chapter 4.4.2).[102]

4.5.2 Prohibition of further public distribution by the BaFin

If the BaFin does not prohibit public marketing of a UCITS before the end of the notification waiting period (see chapter 4.1.4) it may still do so later, and in certain cases is obliged to, after the fund has been admitted for public distribution in Germany.

4.5.2.1 Duty of the BaFin to prohibit further public distribution

The BaFin is bound by law to prohibit the continuation of public marketing and distribution of a UCITS in the following limited circumstances (§133 para (3) InvG), if:

---

[102] See footnote 41, *Begründung, zu Nr.* 114 (§133) *zu Buchstabe g.*

1. in the course of the fund's public marketing, German law provisions which fall outside the scope of the UCITS-Directive as implemented in the Investment Act have been significantly contravened, for example competition law, tax law or banking and financial services law (§133 para (3) no. 2 InvG);

The contravention must be significant for the BaFin to be obliged to prohibit further public marketing of the fund. In defining the significance of the contravention the BaFin should be proportional, balancing the interests of investors and competition in the German investment fund market against the consequences of prohibition for the Management Company and investors.[103] A contravention is always significant if without prohibition investor protection can not be justly restored.

For public marketing to be prohibited the Management Company does not need to have contravened the law, but must at least have had the possibility of influencing the person who contravened the law[104]. If the Management Company distributes funds through a German subsidiary or other agent, it needs to be able to prove it obtained the distributor's contractual confirmation that it holds all necessary licences, maintains the necessary knowhow and observes applicable legal rules for distribution of funds in Germany (see chapters 6.1 and 6.2). It would also be helpful if the Management Company can show that it regularly checks on the activities of its distributors and the fund's other agents in Germany and as a result is in a position to correct obvious deficiencies.

2. the Home Member State Authority has withdrawn the UCITS-authorisation of the fund (§133 para (3) no. 3 InvG);

3. the Management Company has not maintained a German paying and information agent for the fund (see chapter 4.2); and/or

does not accurately name the existing agent in the fund's German simplified and full prospectus (see chapter 4.3.2.3.2) and/or

---

[103] Pfüller/Schmitt in Brinkhaus/Scherer, see footnote 21, §1 AuslInvestmG, note 17.
[104] Pfüller/Schmitt in Brinkhaus/Scherer, see footnote 21, §1 AuslInvestmG, note 18.

does not fulfil certain other notification requirements in the German prospectuses referring to umbrella funds (see chapter 4.3.3.3)

(§133 para (3) no. 4 InvG).

In the cases mentioned in this sub-section 3, the BaFin will grant the Management Company a reasonable time to comply with its statutory duties, but the Management Company is obliged to prohibit further public marketing if it does not cure the deficiency without undue delay after the BaFin's first request.[105]

4.5.2.2 Discretionary power of the BaFin to prohibit further public distribution

In the following limited circumstances the BaFin has discretionary power to prohibit further public marketing (§133 para (4) and (4a) InvG):

1. prior to purchases of units, the Management Company or its distributors do not disseminate prescribed information to German investors (§121 para (1) InvG) (see chapter 6.1);

2. the Management Company does not fulfil its publication duties to investors or its information duties to the BaFin pursuant to §122 para (1) InvG (see chapters 4.4.1 and 4.4.2);

3. the Management Company or its distributors fail to use the German language in any publication concerning the UCITS in Germany pursuant to §123 sentence 1 or 2 InvG (see chapter 6.1.1.4);

4. the Management Company does not pay the BaFin's annual supervision fee punctually (see chapter 4.4.3); or

---

[105] Pfüller/Schmitt in Brinkhaus/Scherer, see footnote 21, §1 AuslInvestmG, note 23.

5. in the case of umbrella funds the Management Company or its distributors publicly market sub-funds in Germany which are not notified to the BaFin for public distribution. In these circumstances, the BaFin has discretionary power to prohibit further public marketing of all sub-funds under the affected umbrella fund, including those notified to the BaFin and which are permitted to be publicly marketed in Germany.

The BaFin must exercise its discretion in accordance with the principles of proportionality and equal treatment of UCITS which are permitted to market their units publicly in Germany. A prohibition order will only be issued if there is no lesser sanction available, and a factor is if the Management Company despite being put on notice by the BaFin does not cure the situation.[106] If the contravention is minor and non-recurring, an admonition by the BaFin might be sufficient to prompt the Management Company to comply. If the breach is serious, sustained or repeated, the BaFin might give the Management Company a warning with a deadline to comply with its legal duties once or, depending on the commitment the Management Company evidences to remedy the situation several times, before it prohibits further public marketing of the fund in Germany. The BaFin will prohibit further public marketing without warning if it considers that the interests of all investors in the fund will be seriously jeopardised.

4.5.2.3 Legal consequences of prohibition of public distribution

4.5.2.3.1 Appeal against prohibition order

A BaFin prohibition order is issued in writing. It contains reasons as well as instructions on rights to appeal.[107] Objections by the Management Company against a prohibition order and legal actions to set it aside, suspend its execution (unless the BaFin orders immediate execution) in cases where the BaFin exercised discretionary power (see chapter 4.5.2.2), but not where the BaFin was bound by law to prohibit further public marketing (see chapter 4.5.2.1) (§133 para (6) InvG). At the Management Company's request, the competent court will institute or revive the suspensive effect of an appeal if the Management Company's marketing and distribution interests outweigh the interests of the German public.[108]

---

[106] Vahldiek in Bödecker, see footnote 22, §133, C. II.

[107] Pfüller/Schmitt in Brinkhaus/Scherer, see footnote 21, §1 AuslInvestmG, note 29.

[108] Pfüller/Schmitt in Brinkhaus/Scherer, see footnote 21, §1 AuslInvestmG, note 29.

4.5.2.3.2 Blocking period for new BaFin notification

The consequence of a prohibition order is that the Management Company is not permitted to notify its intention to market the fund publicly in Germany again until one year has passed after the date of the BaFin order, if the prohibition is made for the reasons outlined in chapter 4.5.2.1 no 1 and in chapter 4.5.2.2 nos 1 to 5. An untimely notification to the BaFin for public marketing of the fund would result in another prohibition order. If the prohibition is made for the reasons outlined in chapter 4.5.2.1 nos 2 and 3 the Management Company is allowed to file a new notification with the BaFin as soon as the situation leading to the prohibition has been remedied. Whenever a new notification is filed, the BaFin notification fee (see chapter 4.3.4.2) has to be paid again.

4.5.2.3.3 Administrative offence

Once the BaFin has issued a prohibition order against a UCITS, the Management Company is only permitted to market the fund in Germany under the narrow private placement rules (see chapter 3). Any public marketing or distribution which is negligently or deliberately undertaken in contravention of the BaFin's prohibition order constitutes an administrative offence, the penalty for which is a fine of up to EUR 100,000 (§143 para (3) no. 27, para (5) InvG). The penalty is meant to exceed any financial gain from the offence. If the fine is lower than the actual gain, the fine can be increased. The penalty is determined by the BaFin after an assessment of the circumstances, including the degree of fault and unlawfulness of the offence, the threat to investor assets and the economic situation of the offender (§17 Administrative Offences Act, *Gesetz über Ordnungswidrigkeiten, OWiG*[109]).

This penalty is directed at any person who markets or distributes the fund in Germany. Representatives of the Management Company or distribution company who disregard the prohibition order may be personally liable. The BaFin can also or in the alternative fine the company represented by such persons (§§8 et seq OWiG). An administrative offence can also be committed through omission, if for example the representative of the Management Company or distribution company fails sufficiently to monitor that only funds permitted for public distribution are in fact marketed in Germany. The offender may appeal to the German courts (§§67 et seq OWiG).

---

[109] http://www.gesetze-im-internet.de/bundesrecht/owig_1968/gesamt.pdf

4.5.2.4 Information by the BaFin

The BaFin informs the Home Member State Authority of the prohibition order. If public marketing has already taken place in Germany, the BaFin will announce the prohibition in the electronic edition of the German Federal Gazette. The Management Company must reimburse the BaFin for the costs it incurred as a result of such announcement (§133 para (7) InvG).

CHAPTER 5 - DISTRIBUTION CHANNELS AND LICENSING REQUIREMENTS

5.1 Distribution through German service providers

In Germany, investment units are distributed through credit institutions and trustee savings banks (*Banken und Sparkassen*), investment management companies (*Kapitalanlagegesellschaft, KAG*), internet platforms, securities and insurance brokers and on stock exchanges.[110]

It is common for foreign Investment Companies to enter into written distribution agreements with German service providers and institutional investors, such as German insurance or investment management companies. Standardised agreements specify fee arrangements, details of how the parties will co-operate, liability, termination, arbitration and/or court jurisdiction.

The Investment Company should obtain the distributor's assurance that it is knowledgeable of and able to comply with the distribution rules for investment funds (see chapter 6.1 for public distribution, see chapter 3 for private placements), rights of revocation and prospectus liability (see chapter 7). The Investment Company should contractually reserve its right to intervene if the distributor engages in unlawful marketing (see chapter 6.2).[111] The distributor will wish to ensure that the Investment Company supplies it promptly with the latest fund documentation and information required by the Investment Act.

The appointment of an independent German distributor does as a rule not avoid the need for the foreign Investment Company to obtain an appropriate distribution licence or EU passport (Article 6b para (5) UCITS Directive).

German fund distributors must be licensed by the BaFin for principal brokering services - the purchase and sale of financial instruments in the institution's own name for the account of others (*Finanzkommissionsgeschäft*, §1 para (1) sentence 2 no. 4 KWG), investment brokering – the brokering business relating to the purchase and sale of financial instruments (*Anlagevermittlung*, §1 para (1a) sentence 2 no. 1 KWG) or contract brokering – the purchase and sale of financial instruments in the name and for the account of others (*Abschlussvermittlung*, §1 para (1a) sentence 2 no. 2 KWG).

---

[110] Baur, see footnote 24, §20, notes 309-313b, 359.

[111] Baur, see footnote 24, §20, note 229.

§34c brokers (§2 para (6) no. 8 KWG), who only require a licence from the local trade authority under §34c GewO, are exempt if they only provide the financial services of investment advice, investment brokering and contract brokering between customers and foreign Investment Companies. Their services are confined to units of foreign investment funds other than hedge funds whose public distribution is permitted under the Investment Act. They are not authorised to acquire ownership or possession of customers' money, fund units or share units in providing such financial services.

German investment management companies are not licensed to privately place foreign investment units which are not permitted for public marketing in Germany (§7 para (2) no. 5 InvG).

5.2 Licence requirements for foreign distributors

5.2.1 UCITS Management Company

In addition to the UCITS product passport (see chapter 2.1.1.1) and the BaFin notification (see chapter 2.1.1.2), the Management Company must have a UCITS Management Company passport to publicly market its funds in Germany. If the Management Company does not intend to sell its units but only to offer other passportable services (individual portfolio management, investment advice, safekeeping and administration for units of collective investment undertakings) in Germany, only the Management Company passport is needed (Articles 6, 6a and 6b UCITS Directive).

Mutual recognition enables a Management Company with its seat in another Member State of the EU or the EEA to provide investment advice and publicly distribute its units for which the notification procedure with the BaFin has been completed through a German branch or cross-border services, without permission from the BaFin, provided that it has been authorised for these activities by the Home Member State Authority with the UCITS Management Company passport. Authorisation granted under the UCITS Directive to a Management Company is valid for all Member States. Only a formal notification procedure needs to be observed in Germany, as summarised in chapters 5.2.1.1 and 5.2.1.2.

Subject to the above conditions, the UCITS Management Company is also permitted to undertake in Germany individual asset management, investment advice, custody, management and public marketing of investment units and other directly connected or ancillary services, and outside the remit of the UCITS Directive, real property funds management (§13 para (1) InvG). Custody of units and public distribution include such services in relation to the UCITS Management Company's own units, third party funds and own or third party non-UCITS funds, provided that they are of German origin or if not are permitted for public marketing in Germany after they have been notified with the BaFin. A licence is not required for private placements of foreign investment units.[112]

Mutual recognition does not apply to establishing a subsidiary of a UCITS Management Company in Germany, which has to apply for a separate banking and/or financial services licence under German law if it engages in licensable banking business or financial services in Germany.[113]

The UCITS Management Company passport does not allow a passported company to establish and manage funds in another Member State. This restriction will change when the UCITS IV Directive replaces the current UCITS Directive. A UCITS fund may then be managed by a Management Company with its registered office in another Member State. A UCITS will be free to designate a Management Company authorised in a Member State other than the UCITS Home Member State in accordance with the relevant provisions of the UCITS IV-Directive. It will be then possible for a German *Kapitalanlagegesellschaft* to establish and manage a Luxembourg Fcp, without as it is the case now being required to set up a Luxembourg subsidiary, by establishing a branch or on a cross-border basis. A fund's UCITS authorisation will no longer be subject to the requirement that it is managed by a Management Company having its registered office in the UCITS Home Member State. The Management Company will not be required to undertake or delegate any activities in the UCITS Home Member State.

UCITS IV further provides that where a Management Company markets the units of the UCITS it manages in a Host Member State without establishing a branch or undertaking any other activities or services in relation to such UCITS, such marketing will only be subject to the UCITS notification procedure in the Host Member State. The notification procedure for the Management Company described in this chapter 5.2.1 will not then be necessary unless the Management Company provides additional passportable services in the Host Member State (Article 16 para (1) UCITS IV Directive). The same will apply when the Management Company distributes units in Germany only through local distributors.

---

[112] Vahldiek in Bödecker, see footnote 22, *Vorbemerkung zu InvG* §§121-127 C. II. 1.
Gesetzentwurf der Bundesregierung Entwurf eines Gesetzes zur Fortentwicklung des Pfandbriefrechts, Deutscher Bundestag Drucksache 16/11130, 16. Wahlperiode, 1.12.2008, Zu Nummer 4 (§2 Abs. 6 KWG), Zu Buchstabe a.
http://dipbt.bundestag.de/dip21/btd/16/111/1611130.pdf
[113] Vahldiek in Bödecker, see footnote 22, *Vorbemerkung zu InvG* §§12, 13, A. II. 1.

5.2.1.1 German branch

The following procedure applies if the UCITS Management Company wishes to have a permanent presence in Germany by opening a place of business to provide services for which it has been authorised (Art. 1a no. 7 of the UCITS Directive). A branch has no separate legal personality from the Management Company.

Art. 6a UCITS Directive provides that any Management Company wishing to establish a branch within the territory of another Member State shall notify the competent authorities of its Home Member State. A notification procedure is needed for each Host Member State where services will be offered. The UCITS Management Company needs to provide the following information and documents to the Home Member State Authority:

1. the Member State within whose territory it plans to establish a branch;

2. its planned programme of operations, comprising the activities and services under Article 5 para (2) and (3) UCITS Directive, and the organisational structure of the branch;

   The branch should put in place an organisational structure enabling it to monitor compliance with applicable German law, including as to insider trading, market abuse and money-laundering

3. the address in the Host Member State from which documents may be obtained; and

4. the names of those responsible for management of the branch.

An EU passported branch must employ at least one manager who fulfils the role of "permanent representative" of the branch. German regulatory law does not prescribe what qualifications such person should have, but relies on the competent Home State Authority's evaluation.

There are no special German regulatory requirements for staffing an EU passported branch. However, to comply with the rules of conduct (§§31 et seq WpHG) and other applicable German laws, the branch should have enough qualified employees to carry out its business, including professionally advising its clients.

Within three months or, under the UCITS IV Directive two months, of receiving the information referred to above the Home Member State Authority will communicate it to the BaFin and inform the Management Company accordingly, unless it doubts the adequacy of the administrative structure or financial situation of the Management Company for the planned activities. The Home Member State Authority will also notify the BaFin of the details of any investor protection compensation scheme. If it refuses to notify such information to the BaFin, the Home Member State Authority has to give reasons to the Management Company within two months of it having received the information. That refusal is subject to the right to apply to the courts in the Home Member State.

Once the Home Member State Authority has informed the BaFin of the planned establishment of a branch in Germany, within two months of receipt of the documents transmitted by the Home Member State Authority, the BaFin will notify the Management Company of the reports the Management Company should make to the BaFin about the branch's planned activity and of German regulatory law which applies to the performance of its proposed activities under the German Banking Act and the German Securities Trading Act (§13 para (4) sentence 1 InvG).[114]

The relevance of other German laws to the branch is a matter for the Management Company.[115] For example, the branch will be subject to German taxation and the German Act on the Detection of Profits from Crimes (*Gesetz über das Aufspüren von Gewinnen aus schweren Straftaten*/GwG). The German Foreign Trade Act (*Außenwirtschaftsgesetz*/AWG) and the Foreign Trade Regulation (*Außenwirtschaftsverordnung*/AWV) impose obligations upon German residents (*Gebietsansässige*) to file reports with the Deutsche Bundesbank for its statistical data collection. German residents include German branches of foreign residents if they are managed from Germany and maintain separate books (§4 para (1) no. 5 AWG).

The branch may be established and commence its activities after receiving notification from the BaFin and at the latest, after expiry of the two months period mentioned above. The regulatory process for registering an EU passported branch should take no more than five months.

The branch should notify the local trade authority of the commencement of its business (§14 GewO). Registration with the local trade authority is made by a standard form. Within

---

[114] For an overview of the applicable provisions in the Banking Act and the Securities Trading Act see Vahldiek in Bödecker, see footnote 22, §13, C. I. 1.

[115] For an overview of other applicable provisions in different German legislation see Vahldiek in Bödecker, see footnote 22, §13, C. I. 3.

three days of filing, the authority will acknowledge receipt of the notification. The local trade authority will forward a copy of this notification to the local tax office. There is no waiting period for its business to commence.

The establishment of a German branch should be registered in the commercial register maintained by the local district court. Registration is not a pre-condition for operations to start, but must take place no later than when operations do start. Registration can take from a few days to several weeks depending on the workload of the court. Registration with the commercial register requires standard corporate documentation to be submitted, including translated and notarised articles. Relevant information must also be updated.

Amendments to the operational plan, especially the branch's proposed activities and organisational structure, its address and who its managers will be, have to be notified in writing to the Home State Authority and the BaFin at least one month before the date on which the amendment becomes effective (§13 para (4) sentence 2 InvG). The Management Company has to inform the BaFin within the same time limit of any changes to the compensation scheme for investor protection in the Home Member State.

5.2.1.2 Cross-border services

Cross-border services for which a BaFin notification is required are "actively" exchanged from abroad into Germany, where the person providing the services does not have a place of business in Germany. An example is customer service representatives from time to time travelling to Germany to advise investors locally. Appointing a German distributor qualifies as active cross-border distribution. "Passive" cross-border services, such as the internet and other forms of distant selling, do not require a UCITS Management Company passport: only a product passport is required.[116]

The procedure described below should be followed if the Management Company engages for the first time in active cross-border distribution of units in Germany. It must deliver the following information to the competent authorities of its Home Member State:

1. the Member State whose territory it intends to operate; and

2. a programme of operations stating planned activities and services (referred to in Article 5 para (2) and (3) UCITS Directive).

---

[116] Vahldiek in Bödecker, see footnote 22, *Vorbemerkung zu InvG* §§ 12, 13, A. II. 4.

The competent authorities of the Home Member State will send this information to the BaFin within one month of receipt. They will also send the BaFin details of any compensation scheme to protect investors.

Within one month of receipt of the information and documents from the Home Member State Authority, the BaFin will inform the UCITS Management Company of German regulatory law which applies to the performance of its proposed activities (§13 para (4) sentence 3 InvG) under the German Banking Act and the German Securities Trading Act.[117] Again, the relevance of other German laws to the branch is a matter for the Management Company.[118]

The UCITS Management Company may provide its services in Germany without waiting for the end of the one month period or receipt of the BaFin's notice.

The Management Company must notify the Home Member State Authority and the BaFin in writing of any amendment to the information referred to in 2. above before implementing it. The notification enables the BaFin to inform the Management Company in sufficient time of any consequential changes in applicable German law.

5.2.1.3 Supervision

If the UCITS Management Company fails to comply with its obligations under German regulatory law, the BaFin will request it to comply within a specified period (§13 para (5) InvG). If the Management Company does not do so the BaFin will inform the Home Member State Authority. If the Home Member State Authority fails to act or if what it does proves insufficient, the BaFin may itself take the necessary actions after informing the Home Member State Authority. The BaFin may prohibit the UCITS Management Company from transacting further business in Germany.

If the matter is urgent the BaFin may take the necessary actions prior to initiating the above procedures. In such circumstances, the BaFin has to inform the Commission and the Home Member State Authority without undue delay (§13 para (6) InvG). The BaFin must amend or suspend its actions if the Commission decides that it should, after it has consulted with the Home Member State Authority and the BaFin.

---

[117] For an overview of the applicable provisions in the Banking Act and the Securities Trading Act see Vahldiek in Bödecker, see footnote 22, §13, C. II. 1.

[118] For an overview of other applicable provisions in different German legislation see Vahldiek in Bödecker, see footnote 22, §13, C. I. 2.

The Home Member State Authority may itself or through agents check any information needed for its regulatory supervision of the branch, after notifying the BaFin (§13 para (7) InvG). If the Home Member State Authority so requests, the BaFin must examine the accuracy of data sent by the Management Company for regulatory purposes to the Home Member State Authority. The BaFin must also permit the Home Member State Authority, an auditor or an expert to inspect such data, and the Management Company is required to allow such inspection.

5.2.2 Securities trading firms passported under the EU banking regulations

The German Banking Act provides in §53b para (1) that a deposit-taking credit institution or securities trading firm which is domiciled in another state of the EEA may conduct banking business or provide financial services in Germany through a branch or by cross-border services without a licence from the BaFin, provided that the enterprise is properly licensed by the authorities in the home state, the business it conducts is covered by the licence and the enterprise is supervised by the appropriate authorities in accordance with European Communities Directives (Directives 89/646/EEC and 93/22/EEC as amended).

5.2.2.1 Notification procedure

The passport notification procedures are similar to those for UCITS Management Companies described in chapter 5.2.1 above. The institution has to notify the competent regulatory authority in its home country of its intention to establish a branch or to provide cross-border services in Germany. After a maximum of three months for establishing the branch and one month for cross-border services, this authority will submit the relevant information to the BaFin and the Deutsche Bundesbank. Receipt by the BaFin triggers a two months review period, at the end of which the BaFin will notify the enterprise of its reporting duties to the BaFin and the Deutsche Bundesbank, and will specify which rules of the German Banking Act apply to performance by the branch of its planned operations in Germany (§53b para (3) KWG). Cross-border services into Germany can start at the earliest when the institution has notified the regulatory authority in its home country.[119] The branch can be established and start its operations in Germany after receipt of the notification from the BaFin, at the latest after expiry of the two month period (§53b para (2) sentence 2 KWG).

---

[119] Leistikow in Günther Luz, Werner Neus, Paul Scharpf, Peter Schneider, Max Weber (editors), Kreditwesengesetz, Kommentar, Stuttgart 2009, §53b KWG, note 18.

In addition to the Banking Act, the institution should inform itself about the provisions of the Securities Trading Act which apply to a branch or cross-border services, applicable German tax law, the Act on the Detection of Profits from Crimes (*Gesetz über das Aufspüren von Gewinnen aus schweren Straftaten*/GwG), the Foreign Trade Act (*Außenwirtschaftsgesetz*/AWG) and the Foreign Trade Regulation (*Außenwirtschaftsverordnung*/AWV), which impose obligations upon German residents (*Gebietsansässige*) including German branches of foreign residents if they are managed from Germany and maintain separate books, to file reports to the Deutsche Bundesbank for its statistical data collection (§4 para (1) no. 5 AWG).[120]

The German branch must notify the local trade authority of the commencement of its business pursuant to §14 GewO, and it should register with the local commercial register maintained by the local district court (see chapter 5.2.1.1).

If the BaFin finds that an enterprise has not complied with applicable provisions of regulatory law, the BaFin will inform the enterprise that it should remedy the breach within a specified period (§53b para (4) KWG). If the enterprise does not comply the BaFin will notify the appropriate authorities of the home state. If the home state authorities fail to take sufficient action, the BaFin, after informing such authorities, may itself take the necessary action. The BaFin may prohibit the enterprise from conducting new business in Germany.

If the matter is urgent the BaFin may take the necessary actions prior to initiating the above procedure (§53b para (5) KWG). In such circumstances, the BaFin has to notify the Commission and the home state authorities immediately. The BaFin must amend or suspend its action if the Commission decides that it should after it has consulted with the home state authorities and the BaFin.

After notifying the BaFin the home state authorities may check or instruct an agent to check the information needed for prudential supervision of the branch (§53b para (6) KWG).

---

[120] Leistikow in Günther Luz, Werner Neus, Paul Scharpf, Peter Schneider, Max Weber (editors), see footnote 119, §53b KWG, note 27.

5.2.2.2 Exemptions

5.2.2.2.1 §2 KWG

§2 KWG contains exemptions from the licence requirements. The most important is for foreign Investment Companies which issue their units in Germany (§2 para (6) 5b KWG).

➢ Non-German Investment Companies by law are treated as not providing licensable financial services if they issue investment units in Germany within the meaning of §2 para (9) InvG.[121] The German legislator has explained that this exception applies to public distributions and private placement of investment units. A licence is, however, required if the Investment Company engages in banking or financial services other than the issuance of investment units.

➢ §2 para (6) no. 8 d) KWG is also important for fund distribution, because it allows German and non-German distributors to market fund units in Germany without a licence, provided that:

- their financial services in Germany consist solely of investment advice (*Anlageberatung*) and investment brokering (*Anlagevermittlung*) or contract brokering (*Abschlussvermittlung*) between German customers and a German or foreign Investment Company; and

- financial services they provide are confined to units issued by German or foreign Investment Companies whose public distribution is permitted under the Investment Act, and they are not authorised to acquire ownership or possession of customer moneys, certificates or units in providing such financial services.

Investment advice (*Anlageberatung*) means making personal recommendations to customers or their representatives for transactions in specific financial instruments, if these recommendations are based on an assessment of the investor's personal circumstances or if the recommendation is presented as suitable for the investor and it is not solely published through information distribution channels or to the public

---

[121] *Gesetzentwurf der Bundesregierung Entwurf eines Gesetzes zur Fortentwicklung des Pfandbriefrechts, Deutscher Bundestag Drucksache 16/11130, 16. Wahlperiode, 1.12.2008, Zu Nummer 4 (§2 Abs. 6 KWG), Zu Buchstabe a.*
http://dipbt.bundestag.de/dip21/btd/16/111/1611130.pdf

(§1 para (1a) sentence 2 no. 1a KWG). For definitions of investment brokering (*Anlagevermittlung*) and contract brokering (*Abschlussvermittlung*) see chapter 5.1.

The above exemption does not extend to privately placed funds, such as single hedge funds.

5.2.2.2.2 Passive freedom to provide services

Another exception is the EU principle of passive freedom to provide services: the right of persons and enterprises with German residence to request services from a foreign provider on their own initiative.[122] Transactions entered into on the unsolicited initiative of the German customer do not require the foreign distributor to be licensed. The freedom to act on the part of recipients of the service is not restricted by regulations relating to the supervision of business.

5.2.3 Distributors without EU passport

5.2.3.1 Exemptions from licence requirement

The exemptions from the licence requirement outlined in chapter 5.2.2.2 also apply to other non-German distributors of investment units. Foreign Investment Companies whose only business in Germany is the public distribution or private placement of their units do not need a banking or financial services licence (§2 para (6) 5b KWG).

A foreign distributor exempted from the licence requirement under the Banking Act may offer units cross-border or establish a local place of business in Germany provided it operates within the applicable exemption. A local place of business requires a trading licence from the local trade authority under §34c GewO and is supervised by this authority. A local place of business is also subject to other German laws, such as tax law and commercial law.

---

[122] *Merkblatt – Hinweise zur Erlaubnispflicht nach §32 Abs. 1 KWG in Verbindung mit §1a KWG von grenzüberschreited betriebenen Bankgeschäften und/oder grenzüberschreitend erbrachten Finanzdienstleistungen,01.04. 2005.*
http://www.bafin.de/cln_161/nn_721290/SharedDocs/Veroeffentlichungen/DE/Service/Merkblaetter/mb__050400__grenzueberschreitend.html?__nnn=true

5.2.3.2 Licence requirement

If none of the exemptions apply, foreign distributors without an EU passport must have a banking or financial services licence from the BaFin to carry out their banking or financial services in Germany. As explained in the BaFin leaflet "Cross-border financial services licensing requirements in Germany"[123], this requirement applies to all providers of banking or financial services domiciled or ordinarily resident abroad which target the German market to offer their services repeatedly and on a commercial basis to enterprises and/or persons domiciled or ordinarily resident in Germany.[124]

Providers from non-EEA states who wish to offer banking and financial services products in Germany must establish a German subsidiary or branch to obtain a banking or financial services licence. The same applies to providers from EEA states which cannot use a European passport for their banking and/or financial services in Germany. If there are several German branches they are deemed to comprise one single institution. The requirements and qualifications for the application procedure are set out in §53 and §32 KWG in connection with §14 of the Regulation on Notifications (*Anzeigenverordnung*).

The enterprise should authorise at least two natural persons residing in Germany to manage the business and represent it, if it conducts banking business or if it provides financial services and is authorised to obtain ownership or possession of funds or securities of customers. These persons are deemed to be the managers of the enterprise. Their names should be reported to and entered in the commercial register.

The institution must keep separate books and deliver corporate accounts to the BaFin and the Deutsche Bundesbank in respect of its business and assets it uses in its business. The provisions of the Commercial Code relating to books of account apply.

The licence may be refused if the BaFin is not satisfied that there will be reciprocity between it and its counterpart in the relevant jurisdiction, on the basis of existing agreements between the two juridictions. The licence will be revoked if the enterprise's licence to conduct banking business or provide financial services has been revoked by the authority responsible for supervising the enterprise abroad.

---

[123] See footnote 122.

[124] The BaFin's view has been confirmed by the European Court of Justice (Judgment of the European Court of Justice (Grand Chamber) of 3 October 2006, Fidium Finanz AG vs Bundesanstalt fur Finanzdienstleistungsaufsicht, case number C-452/04).
http://curia.europa.eu/jurisp/cgi-bin/gettext.pl?where=&lang=en&num= 79938996C19040452&doc=T&ouvert=T&seance=ARRET

The German branch should notify the local trade authority of the commencement of its business to pursuant to §14 GewO, and register with the local commercial register maintained by the local district court (see chapter 5.2.1.1).

The German branch will be subject to German law, including the Banking Act, the Securities Trading Act and the Act on the Detection of Profits from Crimes.

CHAPTER 6 - DISTRIBUTION AND MARKETING RULES

6.1 General rules for public distribution of fund units pursuant to the InvG

The Investment Company and its distributors and intermediaries[125] must observe the distribution rules of §121 InvG before concluding a sales contract with an investor. §121 para (1) InvG requires specific information and documentation to be provided.

6.1.1 Provision of documents before conclusion of a sales contract

6.1.1.1 Purchase of units in UCITS

Before a sales contract for units in a UCITS fund has been concluded, the simplified prospectus for the investment fund must be offered free of charge in its current version and without needing the prior request of the person interested in purchasing fund units (§121 para (1) sentence 1 InvG). In addition and upon request, the full prospectus and the most recent annual and semi-annual report of the investment fund must also be made available free of charge to the person interested in acquiring fund units and to investors (§121 para (1) sentence 2 InvG).

6.1.1.2 Purchase of units in non-UCITS

Before a sales contract for units in a non-UCITS fund has been concluded, the full prospectus and the most recent annual and semi-annual report of the investment fund must be offered in their current version free of charge and without prior request of the person interested in purchasing fund units (§121 para (1) sentence 3 InvG). If a natural person is interested in the acquiring units in a fund of hedge fund or a foreign investment fund comparable to a fund of hedge fund, the additional rules set out in chapter 3.3.1 apply.

6.1.1.3 Rules regarding the fund documentation

The full prospectus must be accompanied by the constitutive documents or it should state where these documents may be obtained free of charge in Germany, from the place of

---

[125] Pursuant to OLG Hamm, Urteil vom 31.01.2000, Az. 31 U 167/97, the duty to provide sales documentation applies to intermediaries in distribution that are actively involved in distributing the fund units as well; LG Frankfurt am Main, Urteil vom 11.10.2005, Az. 2/19 O 401/04, views the duty of intermediaries to provide sales documentation as a contractual obligation arising from the distribution agreement with the Management Company.

business of the information agent in Germany, referred to in the specific information for German investors in the prospectus (see chapter 4.3.2.3.2).

The sales documentation for the investment fund comprising the full prospectus, annual and semi-annual reports, the fund rules or the articles of incorporation and in the case of a UCITS also the simplified prospectus, may be prepared in paper format or stored on a permanent data carrier to which the person interested in the purchase of fund units and existing investors have access. The first alternative is commonly used and means that the Investment Company can provide the information agent and distributors with final documents in electronic format which can be printed out by the information agent and distributors to fulfil requests from investors or other interested parties.

It should be noted that a person interested in purchasing fund units and existing investors may at any time request the sales documentation of the investment fund in paper form. This rule is designed to allow access to the information for parties who do not have adequate electronic means to access or process a non-hard copy format of the documentation.

The potential purchaser of fund units should be advised where in Germany and how the investment fund sales documents may be obtained free of charge. This information should be part of the additional specific information for German investors in the full and simplified prospectus (see chapter 4.3.2.3.2).

The actual purchaser of fund units must receive a duplicate of the subscription form or a statement of purchase containing a statement of the sales charges and redemption fees, and instructions on the purchaser's right of revocation pursuant to §126 InvG (see chapter 7.1.1). The revocation period only starts to run once the subscription form or the contract note has been delivered to the investor.

The additional requirements of §121 para (3) InvG also apply to the public distribution of funds of hedge funds (see chapter 3.3.1).

6.1.1.4 German language

The sales documentation of an investment fund, comprising the full prospectus, constitutive documents, annual and semi-annual reports, subscription form and statement of purchase and in the case of a UCITS also the simplified prospectus, must be in German or accompanied by a German translation. All publications and marketing material must be in the German language or accompanied by a German translation (§123 InvG).

The German version of these documents for non-UCITS investment funds is legally authoritative. For UCITS funds, the German version is only authoritative for investor rights regarding prospectus liability (§127 in connection with §123 sentence 4 InvG).

6.2 Marketing rules for investment funds

Investment funds admitted to public distribution in Germany can be marketed to the public in various ways, for instance by newspapers and gazette publication, marketing flyers and brochures, posters and TV spots.

Various rules have to be observed when selecting how fund units are to be marketed:

- the entity performing the marketing activity must have a regulatory licence which permits it to conduct such activity (see chapter 5);

- the investment fund must be duly registered for public distribution with the BaFin and the registration must be valid and current (see chapter 4); and

- the marketing must comply with applicable law and regulatory provisions for marketing investment fund units, including guidelines issued by the BaFin (see below).

The following provides an overview of the legal and regulatory requirements and guidance issued by the BaFin for marketing.

When reviewing marketing strategies and material, additional rules relating to data protection and general business conditions as well as general civil law may also be relevant.

6.2.1 Most important sources of marketing rules

Important sources for further guidance on marketing are the InvG, in particular §124 InvG, the BaFin Guidelines and the BaFin Marketing Guidelines, and provisions in the WpHG, WpDVerOV and UWG.

UCITS IV will provide additional guidance for UCITS funds. Article 77 of the UCITS IV Directive summarizes key aspects of marketing rules: "All marketing communications to investors shall be clearly identifiable as such. They shall be fair, clear and not misleading. In particular, any marketing communication comprising an invitation to purchase units of UCITS that contains specific information about a UCITS shall make no statement that contradicts or diminishes the significance of the information contained in the prospectus and the key investor information [...]. It shall indicate that a prospectus exists and that the key investor information [...] is available. It shall specify where and in which language such information or documents may be obtained by investors or potential investors or how they may obtain access to them."

6.2.2 Overview of important rules for marketing

6.2.2.1 Availability of prospectuses

All advertising in text form[126] must contain a reference to the prospectuses of the investment fund and where and how they may be obtained (§124 para (1) sentence 1 InvG and BaFin Guidelines VIII. 4. a). Marketing tends to include limited information about the product, and so the recipient of the marketing message must be directed to a point of access to obtain comprehensive information about the investment fund.

This requirement is usually met by stating the name and address of the German information agent and that prospectuses can be obtained at its place of business.

The general rule that all marketing material must refer to the prospectuses and the place where they are available in Germany has often led to the question whether any information for German unitholders, such as notices in newspapers about changes to the investment policy of a fund, already constitute advertising that must state where the prospectuses are available in Germany.

The BaFin has now clarified in no. 12 of the BaFin FAQs that it is not generally necessary to include such a statement. The content of any notice to German unitholders in a foreign investment fund is determined by the content of the requisite notice in the home state of the fund (see chapter 4.4.2.2.2). Accordingly, there is no need for the statement in all unitholder publications.

---

[126] Schmies in Beckmann/Scholtz/Vollmer, see footnote 23, supplement 5/05 – X.05, Vol. 2, §124 InvG, note 6: The reference to 'text form' is borrowed from §126b BGB and includes, for example, marketing by e-mail.

However, if the notice contains information about the availability of specific information or documentation in the home state of the fund, the publication in Germany must state where the respective documentation can be obtained in Germany.[127]

6.2.2.2 Securities indices or derivatives

If the fund rules or articles of association provide for a recognised securities index to be tracked, or that investments will mainly be made in derivatives pursuant to §51 InvG, advertising in relation to the investment fund must contain specific reference to this investment strategy (§124 para (1) sentence 3 InvG and BaFin Guidelines VIII. 4. b).

In contrast to other marketing rules in §124 InvG, this rule applies to all types of advertising, not just advertising in text form, but only to UCITS funds.

6.2.2.3 High volatility

If the composition of the fund or the techniques used for managing it, lead to increased volatility in the performance of the fund, advertising in text form for the fund must include reference to this increased volatility (§124 para (1) sentence 4 InvG and BaFin Guidelines VIII. 4. c). This rules does not apply to non-UCITS funds.

6.2.2.4 Reference to the UWG

The BaFin Guidelines refer to the marketing rules of the UWG. For the marketing of foreign fund units, generally the same rules apply as to German investment funds and therefore the rules of the UWG have to be observed.

§5 UWG deals with misleading commercial activities (*irreführende geschäftliche Handlungen*). Commercial activities are misleading if they contain untrue statements or are based on deceptive information about for example fundamental characteristics of the goods or services advertised, such as advantages, risks and expected results.

---

[127] See also chapter 4.4.2.2.2.

The BaFin Guidelines focus on the following:

> Advertising must not contain statements which mislead investors and suggest a very favourable offer.

> Advertising must not contain a reference to the powers of the BaFin pursuant to the InvG. However, the advertising may refer to the fact that the investment fund in question has been notified to the BaFin and is admitted for public distribution. The BaFin Guidelines cite the following sample wording for such a reference: *"Der Vertrieb der Anteile ist der Bundesanstalt für Finanzdienstleistungsaufsicht nach §132 InvG angezeigt worden."* ("The fund units have been notified to the [German] Federal Financial Supervisory Authority pursuant to §132 InvG.").

> Statements referring to future performance of the investment fund units must not be based on, or make reference to, hypothetical simulations of past performance. Information provided must be based on assumptions backed by objective data. If information is based on gross performance figures, the effect of fees and other costs must be clearly stated.

Statements about future performance must contain clear disclosure about the time period to which they refer, and that past performance, hypothetical simulations or predicted performance are not reliable indicators of future performance.

Statements about past performance must always include a disclaimer that past performance is not a reliable indicator of future performance.[128]

> Advertising may not be linked to references to the risk of inflation or decreasing purchasing power.

> Advertising may not comment on the 'security' of making an investment in the fund units. In general, the word 'security' should be used very cautiously, and only with clarifying additional language.

---

[128] German wording example: *"Die Wertentwicklung in der Vergangenheit ist kein verlässlicher Indikator für die zukünftige Wertentwicklung."*

If it is stated that the investment strategy of the fund is directed at security, this must be clearly placed in the context of the fund's overall investment strategy. The word 'security' should not be featured, nor should the general security of investing into the investment fund in question.

> Advertising should always include a disclaimer as to currency and exchange risks.

6.2.2.5 Marketing rules in the WpHG and WpDVerOV

Although the rules contained in MiFID which are reflected in the WpHG (see chapter 6.2.2.5.1) and the WpDVerOV (see chapter 6.2.2.5.2) and which are further clarified in the BaFin Marketing Guidelines (see chapter 6.2.2.5.3) generally do not apply directly to investment companies[129], these rules can apply to possible German distribution partners of foreign investment funds (see chapter 5), and so should be considered.

The German marketing partner can be asked to confirm that marketing materials provided to it already comply with these rules. Another approach is for the investment fund to produce marketing materials which have no further need of alteration by the marketing partners to achieve more influence on and control over the marketing material handed out to investors and prospective clients.

6.2.2.5.1 Marketing rules in the WpHG

§31 para (2) sentence 1 WpHG requires all information, including marketing material which investment services enterprises (*Wertpapierdienstleistungsunternehmen*[130]) make available to customers, to be fair, clear and not misleading. Marketing material must clearly be recognisable as such (§31 para (2) sentence 2 WpHG).

6.2.2.5.2 Marketing rules in the WpDVerOV

Where information from investment services enterprises including marketing information is addressed to retail clients, §4 WpDVerOV sets out the further requirements that the information must be sufficient for the purpose and presented in a way which makes it understandable for the recipients (§4 para (1) sentence 1 WpDVerOV).

---

[129] MiFID, preliminary note 15 and Article 2 para (1) h).

[130] For a definition see §2 para (4) WpHG in connection with §2 para (3) WpHG.

To comply with the 'fair, clear and not misleading' requirement of §31 para (2) sentence 2 WpHG, the rules in §4 para (1) sentence 2 in connection with para (2) through (11) WpDVerOV require, inter alia, the following:

> If the benefits of an investment service or financial instrument are stated, related risk factors must be clearly disclosed at the same time (§4 para (2) sentence 1 WpDVerOV).

> Statements or warnings which are important must be set out clearly and with due prominence in the information (§4 para (1) sentence 2 WpDVerOV).

> Any comparison of services or products which come within the scope of the rules must be meaningful and balanced, identifying the sources of information, facts and hypotheses (§4 para (3) WpDVerOV).

> Past performance of an instrument, index or service should not be given prominence in the information. Information should also satisfy the following (§4 para (4) WpDVerOV):

- statements as to past performance must include appropriate data for the five preceding years during which the instrument or service was offered or the index was established;

- information for a longer period of time must be presented for periods of twelve months;

- if information is only available for less than five years, data for the period which is available, which must be at least twelve months, should be presented;

- the reference period for any past performance and the sources of information must be clearly stated;

- data in another currency than where the retail client is resident must clearly indicate what the other currency is and warn that the return may increase or decrease because of currency fluctuations; and

- performance based on gross values must disclose the effect of commissions, fees and other charges.

➤ Hypothetical simulations of past performance and any reference to such simulations may only relate to a financial instrument, a reference asset underlying a financial instrument or a financial index. They must be based on actual past performance of at least one financial instrument, reference asset or financial index, the same as or which underlies the relevant financial instrument and must fulfil the aforementioned rules regarding the display of performance set out in §4 para (4) WpDVerOV (§4 para (5) WpDVerOV).

➤ Statements about future performance must not be based on simulated past performance or refer to such simulated past performance. Such statements should be based on reasonable assumptions and objective data. The effect of commissions, fees and other charges must be disclosed clearly if gross values are stated (§4 para (6) WpDVerOV).

➤ Time periods to which the performance data relates should be set out clearly. There should be a disclaimer which states that past performance, hypothetical simulations of past performance and projections of future performance are not a reliable indicator of actual future performance (§4 para (7) WpDVerOV).

➤ Information on specific tax treatment must be accompanied by a warning that the tax treatment will depend on the personal circumstances of the respective client, and may be subject to changes in the future (§4 para (8) WpDVerOV).

6.2.2.5.3 Marketing rules in the BaFin Marketing Guidelines

BaFin has undertaken to further clarify the aforementioned rules and issued the BaFin Marketing Guidelines.

In summary the BaFin Marketing Guidelines refer to the following requirements for marketing communications[131]:

> Any information which is made available to retail clients must be fair, clear and not misleading. Essential statements must be presented in a clear way. Information essential for the retail client must be disclosed.

> The presentation of information must target the group of intended or likely recipients. The information must be sufficient for and it must be presented in an understandable way to the group of recipients to whom the marketing communication is directed. Taking into consideration the average knowledge of the members of such group and the complexity of the product offered, the necessary extent and depth of information given varies.

> The presentation of information must ensure that important statements or warnings are not be disguised or obscured.

> Fairness also requires information to be up-to-date. The timing of updates will depend on the specific case, such as the media used. A clear indication of the date of issuance of the information is recommended and useful.

> When benefits and advantages of an offer are emphasised, the associated risks must be presented and such presentation should be well-balanced.

If performance data is presented taking into account gross values, the effects of commissions, fees and other charges must be set out including all expenses incurred by the client relating to the purchase, holding or sale of the product such as sales commissions, transaction costs and depositary fees. It is considered insufficient to merely indicate on a general level that commissions, fees and other charges will have a negative impact on the performance.[132]

---

[131] The BaFin Marketing Guidelines also contain further details, inter alia, regarding the presentation of performance figures including examples.

[132] BaFin realizes the practical near impossiblity to specify this cost effect for all cases relevant for the recipients of the marketing communications and therefore suggests to take into account the own fee structure of the investment services enterprise charged in similar cases and to supplement the information by providing an internet-based model for the calculation of the net performance. This requirement amongst others of the BaFin Marketing Guidelines is criticised by the fund industry in Germany for being hard to fulfil, in particular in relation to the last requirement mentioned above, and amendments are being discussed.

6.2.3 Prohibition of marketing by the BaFin

The BaFin has the power to prohibit certain types of advertising to prevent abuses (§124 para (3) InvG).

This power was introduced to complement rules under the UWG, and prohibits two types of advertising:

- advertising containing information which misleads investors and suggests a very favourable offer and

- advertising which refers to the powers of the BaFin pursuant to the InvG.

6.2.4 Prohibition of public distribution by the BaFin

The BaFin may also prohibit further public distribution of a foreign investment fund. In the context of advertising, the circumstances in which this will happen are if the investment fund, its representative or a person concerned with the public marketing seriously contravenes the rules in §124 para (1)[133] and (2)[134] InvG, or breaches prohibition orders pursuant to §124 para (3) InvG issued by the BaFin against specific marketing activities (see chapter 6.2.3), and continues with such contraventions despite being warned by the BaFin.

Any such prohibition will be notified by the BaFin in the electronic edition of the German Federal Gazette[135]. The BaFin will also notify the competent bodies of the EU or EEA home state of the investment fund. The person responsible for the breach is obliged to reimburse the BaFin for its costs in connection with these notifications.

If such a prohibition is imposed, the foreign investment fund may only re-file a notification for public distribution one year after the date of the prohibition (see chapter 4.1.5).

---

[133] See chapter 6.2.2.1 – 6.2.2.3.

[134] Dealing with fund of hedge funds.

[135] For further information see: www.ebundesanzeiger.de

6.3 Tax transparency rules

The German regulatory distribution rules and those for tax transparency of investment funds are independent of each other. A fund registered for public marketing is not obliged to fulfil tax transparency requirements and privately placed investment funds are free to apply the tax transparency rules.

The following is a broad overview of tax transparency and taxation rules relating to investment funds. This cannot replace specific tax advice in relation to individual tax cases.

6.3.1 Tax transparent and non transparent investment funds

Investment funds can generally be categorised as tax transparent or non transparent.[136]

Investors in tax transparent funds are taxed on the principle of transparency as if the investment is made directly into the underlying assets, provided that the fund complies with the calculation, reporting and publication requirements in §5 InvStG (see chapter 6.3.2).

At the level of the investment fund, earnings will be determined and attributed to the investor (§2 InvStG). Attribution of earnings differs between distributing and accumulating investment funds, and distributing and accumulating share-classes.

In distributing investment funds, distributed earnings (*ausgeschüttete Erträge*) are as a rule allocated at the time the Investment Company resolves to make the distribution[137]. In accumulating investment funds deemed distributions (*ausschüttungsgleiche Erträge*) are allocated to the investor at the end of the investment fund's fiscal year.[138]

Investment funds which do not fulfil the calculation, reporting and publication requirements set out in §5 para (1) InvStG are designated as non-transparent investment funds. Investors in such funds will be subject to lump-sum taxation (see chapter 6.3.3).

---

[136] The semi-transparent fund status triggering taxation pursuant to §5 para (1) sentence 2 InvStG is based on only partial publication of the relevant tax figures. For further information on the categorisation see Bödecker/Ernst in Bödecker, see footnote 22, §5 InvStG, A.

[137] The resolution must be passed within four months after the fiscal year of the investment fund in order for the investment fund to be categorised as distributing fund (§1 para (3) sentence 5 InvStG).

[138] Bödecker/Ernst in Bödecker, see footnote 22, §5 InvStG, A.

6.3.2 Tax transparency requirements

The investment fund must calculate and publish specific data in order to satisfy the tax transparency requirements. The date on which such data is published will vary according to the nature of the data concerned, whether publications must be effected on each valuation day, once a year or upon the occurrence of certain fiscal events such as distributions.

Submission of data to *WM Datenservice*[139] does not satisfy the publication requirements to qualify for tax transparency status. However, as a practical matter, delivery of data to *WM Datenservice* is relevant for tax purposes and for investor tax certificates, because banks receive information from *WM Datenservice* in connection with the calculation and deduction of withholding tax.

6.3.2.1 Publications on each valuation day

Publications for each valuation day may be made on the internet, in the *elektronischer Bundesanzeiger* or in newspapers published in Germany, as long as they provide for the publication of all relevant data.

On each valuation day, an investment fund's interim profit (*Zwischengewinn*) must be calculated and published, with the redemption price for the investment units. Domestic investment funds within the meaning of §§112 and 113 InvG are exempt from this rule, as are foreign investment funds which are subject to comparable requirements with regard to their investment policy (§5 para (3) sentence 4 InvStG). Special funds are also generally exempted.[140]

The investment fund should calculate income deemed to have been received by a unitholder of foreign fund units after 31 December 1993 and which is not yet subject to withholding tax, and publish a statement of such income, with the redemption price (*akkumulierte thesaurierte Erträge*).

---

[139] For further information, please see www.wmdaten.de

[140] See letter of the *Bundesministerium für Finanzen* (German Ministry of Finance) on the German Investment Tax Act, 18.08.2009.
http://www.bundesfinanzministerium.de/nn_58004/DE/BMF__Startseite/Aktuelles/BMF__Schreiben/Veroffentlichungen__zu__Steuerarten/einkommensteuer/244__a,templateId=raw,property=publicationFile.pdf, note 118 et seq.

The investment fund should also calculate and publish the gain from shares[141] (*Aktiengewinn*) on each valuation day, with the redemption price. The gain from shares is the positive or negative percentage of the value of the fund units attributable to dividend income and realised/unrealised profits/losses from shares held by the fund to the extent that such income has not yet been attributed to investors for tax purposes.

6.3.2.2 Publications once a year

If the fund has paid out distributions in relation to the fiscal year, the annual publication of German tax figures must contain a statement of distributed earnings (§5 para (1) sentence 1 no. 1 InvStG).

The following information should be included in German in relation to a single investment fund unit when a publication is made on each distribution:[142]

- the amount of the distribution (stated to at least four decimal places) and the earnings deemed to have been distributed in previous years which are included in this distribution;

- the amount of distributed earnings (stated to at least four decimal places);

- the extent to which certain other amounts are included in the distributed earnings, such as tax-exempt capital gains[143], capital gains from equities or dividend income.[144]

In addition to information on distribution, the annual German tax publication must contain information and data regarding earnings deemed to have been distributed (*ausschüttungsgleiche Erträge*). Publication must be in German.

The publication must contain a statement on where the annual report[145] in the German language is published or can be obtained.

---

[141] I.e. the equity gain. The publication of these figures is not a requirement (except for special funds) under the tax transparency regime, but a precondition in order for institutional investors holding the investment units as part of their business assets to benefit from other tax privileges. See also Bödecker/Ernst in Bödecker, see footnote 22, §5 InvStG, E.

[142] These are examples, for a list of data to be included please refer to §5 para (1) no. 1 InvStG.

[143] Tax-exempt capital gains pursuant to §2 para (3) no. 1 sentence 1 InvStG in the version in force on 31 December 2008.

[144] For a full list of details to be included please refer to §5 para (1) no. 1 InvStG.

[145] Annual report within the meaning of §45 para (1), §122 para (1) or para (2) of the InvG.

Publication of this information must be accompanied by a certificate of a tax professional authorised to give professional advice[146], an officially recognised accounting firm or a comparable entity, confirming that the information has been determined in accordance with German tax law.

In general, the publication of the aforesaid information has to appear in the *elektronischer Bundesanzeiger* at the latest four months after the fiscal year end of the fund.

If the investment fund resolves to make a distribution in respect of its preceding tax year and such resolution is passed within four months after the end of its fiscal year, the relevant information[147] must be published no later than four months after the date of such resolution.

6.3.2.3 Information upon request

Upon request of the Federal Central Tax Office (*Bundeszentralamt für Steuern*), the investment company must attest to the Federal Central Tax Office as to the correctness of all data[148] published when it makes distributions, in respect of earnings deemed to have been distributed and as to data relating to *akkumulierte thesaurierte Erträge* (see chapter 6.3.2.1), in each case within three months of such request.

6.3.3 Taxation of non-transparent funds

If the investment fund does not comply with the tax transparency requirements[149] set out above, the basis of taxation for an investor in the fund is in respect of any distribution in respect of investment units, interim profit and 70% of the amount by which the last redemption price of an investment unit exceeds the first redemption price determined in the relevant calendar year.

As a minimum, notional income will be assessed of 6% of the last redemption price determined in the relevant calendar year (§6 sentence 1 InvStG).

---

[146] Within the meaning of §3 Tax Advice Act *(Steuerberatungsgesetz)*.
[147] Pursuant to §5 para (1) nos. 1, 2 and 3 InvStG.
[148] Data referred to in §5 para (1) nos. 1, 2 and 4 InvStG.
[149] Set forth in §5 para (1) InvStG.

6.3.4 Relevance of tax transparency

Tax transparency status is determined independently of whether an investment fund is admitted for public distribution in Germany, and applies regardless of the domicile of domestic or foreign investment funds[150].

An investment fund which restricts its marketing to private placement in Germany (see chapter 3) and which is not registered for public marketing may still choose tax transparency. It is doubtful whether non transparent investment funds can be successfully marketed.

Publications required for tax transparency do not amount to public marketing of the investment fund (§2 para (11) no 5 InvG; see chapter 3.1.2.2.5).

An investment fund which may be publicly marketed in Germany is required to comply with ongoing publication requirements, which include publication of issue and redemption prices (§122 para (1) sentence 1 InvG) (see chapter 4.4.2.2.1). Such investment fund may seek tax transparency status by making the relevant additional calculations and publications. The marketing arguments in favour of tax transparent investment funds will also be a relevant consideration.

---

[150] Provided that the foreign investment fund qualifies as an investment fund pursuant to German investment and investment taxation law; for further information please see BaFin circular letter 14/2008 (WA) dated 22 December 2008 on the scope of the applicability of the InvG; http://www.bafin.de/cln_161/nn_721290/SharedDocs/Veroeffentlichungen/DE/Service/Rundschreiben/ 2008/rs__1408__wa.html?__nnn=true and letter of the *Bundesministerium für Finanzen* (German Ministry of Finance) on the German Investment Tax Act dated 18 August 2009 http://www.bundesfinanzministerium.de/nn_58004/DE/BMF__Startseite/Aktuelles/BMF__Schreiben/ Veroffentlichungen__zu__Steuerarten/einkommensteuer/244__a,templateId=raw,property=publication File.pdf

CHAPTER 7 - INVESTOR PROTECTION

7.1 Rights of revocation

7.1.1 §126 InvG – Doorstep sales

§126 InvG provides a right of revocation for doorstep sales. This provision applies to investors' primary purchases of investment units from the Investment Company and to secondary purchases between investors.

The right of revocation presupposes a doorstep sale. The investor must have been induced to buy the units through oral negotiations, including by telephone, outside the permanent business premises of the seller or broker. The right of revocation also applies if the person selling or brokering the sale of units does not have permanent business premises. Inducement to buy is assumed if it cannot be excluded that the negotiations were decisive. Inducement to buy is excluded if the investor had already decided to buy the units before the negotiations had started.[151]

A doorstep sale is also excluded if the seller proves that:

- the purchaser acquired the units in the course of his business operations; or

- the purchaser's visit was prompted by his prior request to negotiate pursuant to §55 para (1) GewO, which resulted in the sale of the units (§126 para (3) InvG).

The purchaser must have invited the seller on his own initiative. However, if the negotiations go beyond what the purchaser requested, his right of revocation is not excluded.[152]

The investor who acquired his interest as a result of a doorstep sale has the right to revoke his agreement to buy the units. The revocation should be in writing to the foreign Investment Company within two weeks of the purported purchase. In the case of a non-UCITS fund the revocation can also be to the German representative. Although the revocation only becomes effective upon receipt of the written revocation, to satisfy the two

---

[151] Vahldiek in Bödecker, see footnote 22, §126 A. III.
[152] Vahldiek in Bödecker, see footnote 22, §126 A. IV.

week period, timely dispatch of the declaration is sufficient (§126 para (2) InvG). The revocation period begins to run once the duplicate of the subscription form or a statement of purchase which contains instructions on the right of revocation satisfying the requirements of §360 para (1) BGB, has been delivered to the investor.[153] The burden of proof for commencement of the revocation period lies with the seller (§126 para (2) sentence 2 InvG).

A revocation declaration in writing requires signature or notarisation (§126 para (1) BGB). The declaration may be in electronic form with a qualifying electronic signature under the German Electronic Signatures Act (§126a para (1) BGB). Fax[154] and e-mail are not sufficient.

The BaFin Guidelines provide wording for the subscription form or statement of purchase pursuant to §126 InvG.

"Right of revocation pursuant to §126 InvG:

If a purchase of investment fund units has been induced by oral negotiations outside the permanent business premises of the party selling the units or brokering their sale, the purchaser may revoke his declaration to purchase said units in a written statement directed to the foreign Investment Company within a period of two weeks (right of revocation); the same applies if the party selling the units or brokering their sale has no permanent business premises. If this involves a distance selling transaction as defined by §312b BGB, then a revocation is precluded when purchasing financial services whose price is subject to fluctuations on the financial market (§312d para (4) no. 6 BGB).

Compliance with the deadline requires only that the declaration of revocation be dispatched in a timely manner. The revocation shall be declared in writing to . . . [name and address of the addressee of the revocation declaration] with name and signature of the individual making the declaration; no reason for the revocation is required.

The revocation period only commences once the duplicate of the subscription form has been handed out to the investor or a statement of purchase has been delivered to the investor, which contains instructions on the right of revocation such as presented here.

---

[153] § 360 BGB in the version of 11.06.2010: see footnote 54.
[154] Vahldiek in Bödecker see footnote 22, §126 B. I; Palandt, see footnote 56, §126 BGB, note 8.

If there is a dispute regarding the start of the period, the burden of proof shall be borne by the seller.

The right of revocation does not exist if the seller can prove that either the purchaser acquired the units within the scope of his business operations

or

that he made a visit to the purchaser, which led to the sale of the units, as a result of a previously-made appointment (§55 para (1) GewO).

If the purchase is revoked and the purchaser has already made payments, the foreign Investment Company is obliged to pay to the purchaser, if necessary matching payment with delivery, the costs paid and an amount equivalent to the value of the units paid for on the day after the receipt of the declaration of revocation.

The right of revocation may not be waived."

***

"Widerrufsrecht gemäß §126 InvG:

Erfolgt der Kauf von Investmentanteilen durch mündliche Verhandlungen außerhalb der ständigen Geschäftsräume desjenigen, der die Anteile verkauft oder den Verkauf vermittelt hat, so kann der Käufer seine Erklärung über den Kauf binnen einer Frist von zwei Wochen der ausländischen Investmentgesellschaft gegenüber schriftlich widerrufen (**Widerrufsrecht**); dies gilt auch dann, wenn derjenige, der die Anteile verkauft oder den Verkauf vermittelt, keine ständigen Geschäftsräume hat. Handelt es sich um ein **Fernabsatzgeschäft** i. S. d. §312b des Bürgerlichen Gesetzbuchs, so ist bei einem Erwerb von Finanzdienstleistungen, deren Preis auf dem Finanzmarkt Schwankungen unterliegt (§312d Abs. 4 Nr. 6 BGB), ein Widerruf ausgeschlossen.

Zur Wahrung der Frist genügt die rechtzeitige Absendung der Widerrufserklärung. Der Widerruf ist gegenüber ..., (hier bitte Namen und Anschrift desjenigen, gegenüber dem der Widerruf zu erklären ist, einsetzen) schriftlich unter Angabe der Person des Erklärenden einschließlich dessen Unterschrift zu erklären, wobei eine Begründung nicht erforderlich ist.

Die Widerrufsfrist beginnt erst zu laufen, wenn die Durchschrift des Antrags auf Vertragsabschluss dem Käufer ausgehändigt oder ihm eine Kaufabrechnung übersandt worden ist und darin eine Belehrung über das Widerrufsrecht wie die vorliegende enthalten ist.

Ist der Fristbeginn streitig, trifft die Beweislast den Verkäufer.

Das Recht zum Widerruf besteht nicht, wenn der Verkäufer nachweist, dass entweder der Käufer die Anteile im Rahmen seines Gewerbebetriebes erworben hat
oder
er den Käufer zu den Verhandlungen, die zum Verkauf der Anteile geführt haben, auf Grund vorhergehender Bestellung gemäß §55 Abs. 1 der Gewerbeordnung aufgesucht hat.

Ist der Widerruf erfolgt und hat der Käufer bereits Zahlungen geleistet, so ist die ausländische Investmentgesellschaft verpflichtet, dem Käufer, gegebenenfalls Zug um Zug gegen Rückübertragung der erworbenen Anteile, die bezahlten Kosten und einen Betrag auszuzahlen, der dem Wert der bezahlten Anteile am Tage nach dem Eingang der Widerrufserklärung entspricht.

Auf das Recht zum Widerruf kann nicht verzichtet werden. "

For an investment fund which is legally not independent, the expression "Investment Company" in the preceding text should be substituted by "Management Company".

If the right of revocation is printed on the back of the subscription form and/or statement of purchase, the front page should include a prominent statement to that effect.

If the revocation takes place after the purchaser has already made a payment, the foreign Investment Company must pay the purchaser what the purchaser paid plus an amount corresponding to the value of the paid units on the day following receipt of the declaration of revocation if applicable, in return for transfer of the acquired units.

The right of revocation cannot be waived by the purchaser or contracted out by the seller.

It is excluded if the purchase is a distance selling transaction as defined by §312b BGB (see chapter 7.2.2.1) of financial instruments whose price is subject to financial market fluctuations (§312d para (4) no. 6 BGB), which is typically the case for investment units.

7.1.2 Other rights of revocation and rescission

In addition to the right of revocation contained in §126 InvG, the German Civil Code provides for additional revocation and rescission rights. However, as regards foreign Investment Companies, German investors only benefit from these rights of revocation and rescission if under conflict of law rules German civil law applies to the contractual relationship between investor and Investment Company (see chapter 7.3.3.1.1).

The rights of revocation for consumers under the German Civil Code do not apply to the purchase of investment units. §312 BGB gives consumers a right of revocation for doorstep sales. However, §126 InvG is *lex specialis* and supersedes §312 BGB in relation to publicly marketed funds (§312a BGB) (for private placements see chapter 3.3.3.2). §312 d BGB gives consumers a right of revocation for distance contracts but does not apply to the sale of investment units (see chapter 7.1.1).

The German Civil Code provides rights of rescission (*Anfechtungsrechte*) which allow a contracting party to avoid its declaration to enter into the contract on the grounds of mistake, deceit or duress. The purchaser can rescind its declaration to buy units for mistake on the grounds that the Investment Company breached its information duties (see chapter 7.3.3.1). Rescission of a contract results in mutual restitution. It might also give rise to claims for damages through reliance on the validity of the contract.

The investor may have a claim for damages against the Investment Company or the distributor for breach of its precontractual or contractual obligation to disclose information or to advise the investor. The claim may also be based on the Investment Company's or distributor's breach of information duties (see chapter 7.3.3.1).

7.2 Consumer information

§§312 et seq BGB impose information duties on entrepreneurs from which no derogation is permitted to disadvantage the consumer or customer. These provisions apply to the distribution of investment funds.

7.2.1 Applicability of German consumer protection law

As far as foreign Investment Companies and fund distributors are concerned, German consumer protection law follows the EU Regulation on the law applicable to contractual obligations[155] which applies directly in Germany. This EU Regulation provides that a contract concluded by a natural person (the consumer) for a purpose outside his trade or profession with another person (the professional) acting in the exercise of his trade or profession shall be governed by the law of the country where the consumer has his habitual residence, provided that the professional:

1. pursues his commercial or professional activities in the country where the consumer has his habitual residence or

2. directs such activities by any means to that country or to several countries including that country, and the contract falls within the scope of such activities.

These conditions should be satisfied if investment units are offered to German investors by foreign distributors. German consumer protection law should therefore apply whenever fund units are distributed to consumers by foreign distributors in Germany.[156]

Regulation (EC) No 593/2008 also provides that the parties to a consumer contract may choose the applicable national law. Their choice may not, however, deprive the consumer of the protection afforded by provisions of law in the country where he has his habitual residence which cannot be excluded by mutual agreement. Consequently, the German rules for consumer protection contained in §§305 et seq BGB (for standard business terms) and §§312b-312f BGB (for consumer contracts) will still apply, notwithstanding applicable foreign contract law.

---

[155] Regulation (EC) No 593/2008 of the European Parliament and of the Council of 17 June 2008 on the law applicable to contractual obligations (Rome I).
http://eur-lex.europa.eu/LexUriServ/LexUriServ.do?uri=OJ:L:2008:177:0006:0016:EN:PDF

[156] German consumer law is not applicable to the investment management contract between the Investment Company and the consumer because Regulation (EC) No 593/2008 provides an exception, inter alia, for the subscription and redemption of units in collective investment undertakings in so far as these activities do not constitute provision of a financial service as referred to in sections A and B of Annex I to Directive 2004/39/EC. The contractual relationship established between the issuer or the offeror and the consumer should not necessarily be subject to the mandatory application of the law of the country of habitual residence of the consumer, as there is a need to ensure uniformity in the terms and conditions of an issuance or an offer. The rationale of this exception is to ensure that rights and obligations which constitute a financial instrument are not regulated by different laws which could change their nature and prevent their fungible trading and offering.

7.2.2 Distance contracts

The rules of the German Civil Code relating to distance contracts *(Fernabsatzverträge)* implement Directive 97/7/EG concerning consumer protection and the formation of contracts by telecommunication, and Directive 2002/65/EC[157] concerning the distance marketing of consumer financial services, amending Council Directive 90/619/EEC and Directives 97/7/EC and 98/27/EC.[158]

If the purchase of investment units qualifies as a distance contract, the Investment Company and/or distributor are subject to duties to provide information under the German Civil Code.

7.2.2.1 Definition of distance contract

According to §312b para (1) BGB, distance contracts are concluded B2C between a natural or legal person or a partnership with legal personality (entrepreneur) which when entering into a legal transaction acts for the purpose of its trade, business or profession and a natural person (consumer) who enters into a legal transaction for a purpose outside his trade, business or profession.

Distance contracts include contracts to supply banking and financial services, such as the brokering of investment units[159] which are entered into solely by distance communication through a distance sales system. Distance communication is defined in §312b para (2) BGB as a means of communication which can be used to initiate or to enter into a contract without the simultaneous physical presence of the contracting parties, including letters, catalogues, telephone calls, faxes, e-mails and radio, tele and media services.

7.2.2.2 Information duties

If the purchase of investment units qualifies as a distance contract under §312c BGB, the distributor has the following information duties to the investor:

---

[157] Directive 2002/65/EC of the European Parliament and of the Council of 23 September 2002 concerning the distance marketing of consumer financial services and amending Council Directive 90/619/EEC and Directives 97/7/EC and 98/27/EC.
http://eur-lex.europa.eu/LexUriServ/LexUriServ.do?uri=OJ:L:2002:271:0016:0024:EN:PDF

[158] Directive 97/7/EG of the European Parliament and the Council of May, 20, 1997 concerning consumer protection as to the formation of contracts by telecommunication (Official Gazette EG no. L 144 p. 19).
http://eur-lex.europa.eu/LexUriServ/LexUriServ.do?uri=CELEX:31997L0007:EN:HTML

[159] Palandt, see footnote 56, §312b BGB, note 10b.

At the beginning of any telephone conversation initiated by him, the entrepreneur has to expressly identify himself and his business purpose (§312c para (2) BGB).

In good time before the consumer makes his contractual declaration, the distributor must in a manner appropriate to the means of distance communication clearly, comprehensibly and stating his business purpose, provide the information specified in Article 246 §§1 and 2 EGBGB.

In the case of financial services, the entrepreneur must also provide the consumer in text form (see chapter 7.2.2.3) with the contractual terms, including standard business terms, and the information specified in Article 246 §§1 and 2 EGBGB in good time before the consumer makes his contractual declaration. If, at the request of the consumer, the contract is entered into by telephone or using another means of distance communication which does not allow for text form, the entrepreneur must provide this information without undue delay after the distance contract is entered into (Article 246 §2 para (1) EGBGB).

The following information is required to be provided pursuant to Article 246 §§1 and 2 EGBGB in good time before the consumer makes his contractual declaration:

1. The entrepreneur's identity, including the public business register where the legal entity is registered, and its register number or equivalent identification;

2. The identity of a representative agent in the Member State in which the consumer has his residence if the entrepreneur has such an agent, or the identity of another person engaged in commerce other than the entrepreneur if the consumer is doing business with such person, and the capacity in which such person acts in its dealings with the consumer;

3. The entrepreneur's delivery address and any other address which is of importance for the business relationship between the entrepreneur, his representative agent or another person engaged in commerce within the meaning of no. 2 above and the consumer. In the case of corporations, associations and groups of persons the name of an authorised representative should also be provided[160];

---

[160] If this information is contained in the contractual terms including general terms and conditions, it has to be clearly marked and configurated, see Article 246 §2 para (3) sentence 2 EGBGB.

4. The essential characteristics of the contractual services and information on how the contract enters into force;

5. The minimum duration of the contract, if it contains continuous or periodic services;

6. Any reservation to perform a[nother] service, which is equivalent in quality and price, and a reservation not to perform the contractual services at all if they are not available;

7. The total price of the services, including all price components and taxes charged to the entrepreneur's account or, if the exact price cannot be stated, how it is calculated in such a way to enable the consumer to check the price;

8. If applicable, any additional mailing and shipping expenses and an indication of possible additional taxes and expenses which are not charged to the entrepreneur's account or invoiced by him;

9. The details of payment and delivery or performance;

10. The existence or non-existence of a right of revocation or return and the conditions and details of how the right is performed, in particular the name and address of the respondent, and the legal consequences including information on the amount, if any, which the consumer has to pay for the service which has been delivered in circumstances where the right of revocation or return is exercised (§357 para (1) BGB)[161];

11. Any additional costs which the consumer is required to pay to use the instrument of distance communication, if such additional costs are charged by the entrepreneur;

12. Any time limit during which information which has been provided remains valid. For example, if the offer, particularly with regard to pricing, is temporary.

---

[161] If this information is contained in the contractual terms including general terms and conditions, it has to be clearly marked and configurated, see Article 246 §2 para (3) sentence 2 EGBGB.

In the case of distance contracts relating to financial services, the following additional information has to be made available:

13. The entrepreneur's main business operations and the regulatory authority responsible for the entrepreneur's licence;

14. If applicable, a statement that the financial service refers to financial instruments which due to their characteristics or procedures intrinsic to them bear specific risks or are subject to financial market price fluctuations over which the entrepreneur has no influence, and a statement that earnings in the past do not indicate future earnings;

15. The contractual terms for termination, including possible contractual penalties[162];

16. The laws of the EU Member States which the entrepreneur takes as the basis for his precontractual relationship with the consumer;

17. A contractual clause on the governing law or the competent court in relation to the distance contract;

18. The language(s) in which the contractual terms and information to be provided to the consumer before the distance contract is concluded are stated and the language(s) in which the entrepreneur undertakes to communicate, with the consumer's consent, during the life of the contract;

19. How the consumer may bring an out of court complaint and seek remedies and, if necessary, what conditions apply to such action; and

20. The existence of a guarantee fund or other compensation regulations, which are not covered by the Directive 94/19/EC of the European Parliament and of the Council of 30 May 1994 on deposit guarantee schemes (ABl. EG Nr. L 135 S. 5) and Directive 97/9/EC of the European Parliament and of the Council of 3 March 1997 on investor compensation schemes (ABl. EG Nr. L 84 S. 22).

---

[162] If this information is contained in the contractual terms including general terms and conditions, it has to be clearly marked and configurated, see Article 246 §2 para (3) sentence 2 EGBGB.

Article 246 §1 para (3) EGBGB makes an exception for telephone communications. The entrepreneur only has to inform the consumer according to nos. 1-12 above, whereupon a notice under no. 3 is only necessary if the consumer has to make a prepayment, provided that the entrepreneur has informed the consumer that upon his request further information and of what sort will be made available, and if the consumer has expressly opted out of receiving further information before declaring his intention to contract.

7.2.2.3 Text form

If text form is prescribed by law, the declaration must be made in a document or another manner suitable for it to be permanently reproduced in writing. The person making the declaration must be named and completion of the declaration must be evidenced by the reproduction of a signature of the name or in some other way (§126b BGB). For example, letter, fax, e-mail, disc and CD-Rom are suitable media for text form.[163] Before information is transmitted, the entrepreneur should make sure that the consumer agrees to how material information is to be communicated electronically.[164] Merely making the information available on the entrepreneur's website will not be sufficient, because the entrepreneur would need to prove that the consumer downloaded the information in a timely manner.[165]

7.2.3 Electronic business dealings

§312e BGB, which implements the Directive on electronic commerce[166] into German law, sets out information requirements for electronic business dealings. Such information duties are addressed at entrepreneurs and customers. They apply B2C and B2B, but not C2C.[167]

If an entrepreneur uses a tele service or media service in order to enter into a contract for the supply of goods or services (e-commerce contract), he must provide the customer with reasonable, effective and accessible technical means by which the customer may identify and correct input errors prior to making his order (§312e para (1) no. 1 BGB).

---

[163] Palandt, see footnote 56, §312c BGB, note 7.
[164] Palandt, see footnote 56, §312c BGB, note 7.
[165] Palandt, see footnote 56, §312c BGB, note 7.
[166] Directive 2000/31/EC of the European Parliament and of the Council of 8 June 2000 on certain aspects of information society services, in particular electronic commerce, in the Internal Market http://eur-lex.europa.eu/LexUriServ/LexUriServ.do?uri=CELEX:32000L0031:EN:HTML
[167] Palandt, see footnote 56, §312e BGB, note 3.

The entrepreneur has to notify the customer clearly and comprehensibly of the information specified in Article 246 §3 EGBGB in good time prior to sending his order (§312e para (1) no. 2 BGB) as follows:

1. each technical step which leads to the conclusion of a contract;

2. if the wording of the contract is saved by the entrepreneur after conclusion of the contract and how the customer can access it;

3. how the customer can obtain notice of and correct input errors before placing his order and the technical steps to make such correction;

4. the language(s) in which a contract can be concluded; and

5. all relevant codes of good conduct to which the entrepreneur adheres and how electronic access to these codes may be obtained.

The entrepreneur has to confirm receipt of the order without undue delay by electronic means for the customer (§312e para (1) no. 3 BGB). The order and the acknowledgement of receipt are deemed to have been received if the parties for whom they are intended are able to retrieve them in normal circumstances.[168]

These rules do not apply if the contract is entered into exclusively by personal electronic communication, for instance if parties who are not consumers have exchanged e-mails or otherwise come to a contractual agreement (§312e para (2) BGB).

The entrepreneur must make it possible for the customer to retrieve the contract terms, including the standard business terms, when the contract is entered into and to save them in a form which allows them to be reproduced (§312e para (1) no. 4 BGB).

The more extensive duties to provide information under other provisions are unaffected (§312e para (3) BGB). If the customer has a right of revocation, the revocation period does not start until the information duties stated above are complied with in text form.

---

[168] Palandt, see footnote 56, §312e BGB, note 7.

7.3 Prospectus liability

7.3.1 §127 InvG

7.3.1.1 Inaccurate or incomplete information

The Investment Act allows investors in Germany to claim compensation if information contained in the full or simplified sales prospectus is inaccurate or incomplete, provided that the information is of material significance in evaluating the fund units. Such information must be accurate and complete when the units are purchased and at the time the offer is made, if offer and acceptance follow one another.

The term "information" includes facts, value judgments and forward-looking statements.[169] Value judgments and forward-looking statements must be based on facts and must be commercially justifiable.[170]

Information is of material significance if its inaccuracy or incompleteness can seriously and adversely affect the investor's investment position. It is also of material significance if the information, provided that it was accurate and complete, is qualified such that the investor would refrain from purchasing units.[171] Information which an ordinary investor would on balance take into consideration is relevant.[172]

Information is inaccurate if it is untrue, exaggerated, ambiguous, vague or is true verbatim whilst creating a deceptive overall picture. The prospectus must be up-to-date. New factual circumstances can render old facts inaccurate. Information is incomplete if material parts are entirely or partly missing, for example if relevant circumstances are not described comprehensively.[173] The prospectus as a whole must give a true picture of the fund and its material risks.[174] Important information must not be typographically put in the background.

---

[169] BGH, Urteil vom 12.07.1982, Az. II ZR 175/81, WM 1982, 862, 865.

[170] Schödermeier/Baltzer in Brinkhaus/Scherer, see footnote 21, §20 KAGG, note 6.

[171] Baur, see footnote 24, §20 KAGG, note 9.

[172] BGH, Urteil vom 12.07.1982, Az. II ZR 175/81, WM 1982, 862, 865; Schödermeier/Baltzer in Brinkhaus/Scherer, see footnote 21, § 20 KAGG, note 5.

[173] Vahldiek in Bödecker, see footnote 22, §127, A. II.

[174] Schmies in Beckmann/Scholtz/Vollmer, see footnote 23, supplement 4/07 – VI.07, Vol. 2, §127 InvG, note 9.

The viewpoint of an average investor who reads the prospectus diligently and with care is decisive. Obvious mistakes such as typing errors are irrelevant.[175] Describing fund units disadvantageously does not lead to inaccuracy within the meaning of §127 InvG.[176]

Examination and acceptance of a foreign investment fund's prospectus by the competent home regulator has no bearing on its accuracy or completeness in the meaning of §127 InvG. Accuracy and completeness are assessed on the basis of German law, except in the case of the simplified prospectus. According to §127 para (2) InvG the content of the simplified prospectus of a German UCITS fund is determined only by §42 para (2) to (4) InvG. For foreign UCITS funds the German legislator has explained that they shall only be subject to the laws of their Home Member State (in conjunction with Annex 1 Schedule C of the UCITS-Directive and the recommendations of the Commission 2004/384/EC of 27 April 2004[177]).[178]

7.3.1.2 Units purchased on the basis of the prospectus

Prospectus liability pursuant to §127 InvG requires that the units have been purchased on the basis of the deficient full or simplified prospectus.

Purchase on the basis of the document does not require a causal link between the purchase and the inaccurate or incomplete information.[179] Instead it limits the universe of claimants to primary investors who acquire their units from the Investment Company through a distributor or other agent, who by law is required to offer the simplified prospectus and to make the full prospectus available to investors (§121 para (1) sentences 1 and 2 InvG) (see chapter 6.1.1). This excludes secondary purchasers, because they acquire their units from a primary investor.

Investors in privately placed funds are also excluded from being claimants under §127 InvG, because the Investment Act does not apply to private placements and a prospectus does not need to be made available to them (see chapter 3.3). If such investors have nevertheless obtained a prospectus, they might be able to base a claim for prospectus liability on general civil law principles (see chapter 7.3.3). Investors in foreign hedge funds may be entitled to make a claim under §127 InvG, because their private placement is

---

[175] Schödermeier/Baltzer in Brinkhaus/Scherer, see footnote 21, §20 KAGG, note 7.

[176] Schödermeier/Baltzer in Brinkhaus/Scherer, see footnote 21, §20 KAGG, note 7.

[177] http://eur-lex.europa.eu/LexUriServ/LexUriServ.do?uri=CELEX:32004H0384R(01):EN:HTML

[178] See footnote 41, *Begründung, zu Nr. 109 (§127)*.

[179] Vahldiek in Bödecker, see footnote 22, §127, A. III.

regulated by the Investment Act and a prospectus accordingly needs to be provided to them (see chapter 3.3.1).[180]

It is not necessary that the investor has accepted the prospectuses or printed relevant documents from the internet, or even that the investor has read them.[181] The investor does not need to be aware of correct or additional information which should have been contained in the prospectus. The contract of purchase does not need to be valid, irrevocable or incontestable.

A different view is that the words "on the basis of the prospectus" require a causal link such that the investor must have taken note of the prospectus in general terms.[182] The prospectus must have been a part of the investor's decision-making process but not necessarily the main part. According to this view, there is no claim if the investor made its investment decision completely independently of the prospectuses. However, if the investor can prove that the prospectus was inaccurate or incomplete at the time of purchase, this view assumes that the investor based its investment decision on the prospectus. It is then up to the respondent to prove the contrary.

7.3.1.3 Respondents and standard of care

Prospectus liability under §127 InvG can only be established against the foreign Investment Company and its authorised distributors.

Claims for prospectus liability can lie against the foreign Investment Company and any person who sold the units in its own name on a commercial basis (§127 para (1) sentence 1 InvG). Such a respondent will not be held liable if it was not aware of the inaccuracy or incompleteness of the sales prospectus and such lack of awareness was not the result of gross negligence (§127 para (3) sentence 1 InvG). The burden of proof is reversed and in this case lies with the respondent.

Any person who on a commercial basis, brokers the sale of units or sells units in the name of someone else can be held liable, provided that such person was aware of the inaccuracy or incompleteness of the sales prospectus (§127 para (4) sentence 1 InvG). Here too the burden of proof is reversed, so that in this case the respondent has to demonstrate its lack

---

[180] Vahldiek in Bödecker, see footnote 22, *Vorbemerkung zu InvG* §§ 121-127, C. I. 3.

[181] Vahldiek in Bödecker, see footnote 22, §127, A. III; Schmies in Beckmann/Scholtz/Vollmer, see footnote 23, supplement 4/07 – VI.07, Vol. 2, §127 InvG, notes 10 et seq.

[182] Schödermeier/Baltzer in Brinkhaus/Scherer, see footnote 21, §20 KAGG, notes 9 and 10; Baur, see footnote 24, §20 KAGG, notes 14 and 15.

of awareness. Unlike the previous group of respondents, gross negligence with regard to the inaccuracy or incompleteness does not enable a claim to be made against these respondents.

All respondents who are found to be liable are treated as joint and several debtors. The investor at its discretion can claim full restitution from each debtor, but only once. The debtors are obliged to compensate each other in accordance with their individual degree of responsibility.[183]

7.3.1.4 Investor's knowledge

A claim will not exist if the investor at the time of the purchase was aware of the inaccuracy or incompleteness of the sales prospectus (*volenti non fit iniuria*). The burden of proof in these circumstances lies with the respondent.

According to one opinion it is not sufficient that the respondent only proves that the investor was aware of the matters that should have been included in the prospectus or which should have been stated accurately. The investor must also know that the prospectus is inaccurate.[184]

The preferable view is that there is no prospectus liability if the investor was on notice of the true circumstances at the time of purchase, irrespective of the investor being aware that the prospectus was inaccurate.[185] Such an investor does not need protection because it would contradict such investor's previous behaviour (*venire contra factum proprium*), if the investor purchased the units in knowledge of the true circumstances and then claimed damages for not being put on notice of the very same circumstances. The investor would be able to speculate on the value of the units, returning units for prospectus liability if prices fall and keeping the units if prices rise.

7.3.1.5 Scope of liability

The investor may demand that any of the joint and several debtors acquire its units in return for reimbursement of the issue price paid by the investor.

---

[183] Vahldiek in Bödecker, see footnote 22, §127, A. VI.
[184] Schmies in Beckmann/Scholtz/Vollmer, see footnote 23, supplement 4/07 – VI.07, Vol. 2, §127 InvG, note 17; Baur, see footnote 24, §20 KAGG, note 28.
[185] Schödermeier/Baltzer in Brinkhaus/Scherer, see footnote 21, §20 KAGG, note 22.

If the investor at the time it becomes aware of the inaccuracy or incompleteness of the sales prospectuses no longer holds the units, it may demand payment of the amount by which the issue price paid exceeds the redemption price of the units at the time of disposal. How the investor disposed of its units, whether through a sale, gift or otherwise, is irrelevant. According to one opinion this applies even if the investor disposes of the units after becoming aware that the prospectus is inaccurate.[186] The prevailing view, however, is that the investor forfeits its claims derived from prospectus liability in these circumstances.[187]

Reimbursement includes any damage through or loss incurrd by relying on the validity of the purchase. This comprises the issue price and any additional expenses, such as issue surcharges, management fees and commissions.[188] The investor is allowed to keep any benefits, such as dividend payments. The debtor on the other hand cannot set-off its costs and fees.

7.3.1.6 Limitation of claim

A claim under §127 InvG becomes statute-barred one year after the date on which the purchaser became aware of the inaccuracy or incompleteness of the sales prospectus, and at the latest three years after conclusion of the purchase contract (§127 para (5) InvG). For the Investment Company and its distributors, it is therefore important to keep a record of the date of the purchase, being the date on which the investor's offer was accepted.

7.3.2 §44 Stock Exchange Act

Investors in Exchange Traded Funds are barred from claiming compensation for prospectus liability pursuant to §44 BörsG. This is because no listing prospectus is required for admission of foreign investment funds within the meaning of the Investment Act to the Regulated Market of a German stock exchange (§32 para (3) no. 2 BörsG in connection with §1 para (2) no. 1 WpPG) (see chapter 8.2.2.5). The Investment Company is not even permitted to voluntarily prepare a listing prospectus (§1 para (2) no. 1 and para (3) WpPG). The issuance of a listing prospectus is, however, a mandatory requirement for a claim pursuant to §44 BörsG.[189]

---

[186] Vahldiek in Bödecker, see footnote 22, §127, A. VI.

[187] Schödermeier/Baltzer in Brinkhaus/Scherer, see footnote 21, §20 KAGG, note 28; Schmies in Beckmann/Scholtz/Vollmer, see footnote 23, supplement 4/07 – VI.07, Vol. 2, §127 InvG, note 23.

[188] Vahldiek in Bödecker, see footnote 22, §127, A. VI.

[189] Gross, Kapitalmarktrecht, München 2009, §44 BörsG, note 23 et seq.

7.3.3 Civil law

In addition to §127 InvG, investors can base a claim on general civil law principles.[190]

7.3.3.1 Contract

In relation to a foreign Investment Company or distributor, German investors only benefit from contractual claims for damages if under conflict of law rules, German law applies to the contractual relationship between the investor and such company or person.

7.3.3.1.1 Legal relationship between investor and Investment Company

The contractual relationship between investors habitually resident in Germany and a foreign Investment Company is generally governed by the law of the home state of the Investment Company.

Investment fund in corporate form

If the foreign investment fund is set up as a corporation, such as a Luxembourg Sicav or an Irish plc, the law governing the relationship between the fund and its shareholders is the law of the company's seat or place of incorporation (incorporation versus company seat theory).[191] For UCITS, which under Art. 3 of the UCITS-Directive are required to have their registered seat in the same Member State as their head office, this is the law of the company seat. German contract law does not apply because the investor is a shareholder and not a recipient of contractual services.

Investment fund in contractual form

If the foreign investment fund is set up in contractual form, such as a Luxembourg Fcp, United Kingdom unit trust or common fund, the relationship between the investor and the Investment Company is subject to the law of contract. Investors who purchase fund units usually enter into an investment management agreement with the foreign Investment Company. The investor may have claims for damages against the foreign Investment

---

[190] According to Schmies in Beckmann/Scholtz/Vollmer, see footnote 23, supplement 4/07 – VI.07, Vol. 2, §127 InvG, note 29, §127 InvG supersedes liability claims on general civil law principles. According to this view such liability claims are only applicable if other documents than the full and simplified prospectus in the sense InvG are concerned.

[191] Einsele, Bank- und Kapitalmarktrecht Nationale und Internationale Bankgeschäfte, Tübingen 2006, §10 Investmentgeschäft, note 56.

Company pursuant to §280 para (1) BGB for breach of this agreement. Such claims may arise, for example, if the investor suffers a loss because the fund's assets are not invested in accordance with its management regulations and prospectus, provided that German contract law is applicable.

As a rule, the investment management agreement contains a choice of law clause, typically referring to the law of the country in which the fund is set up and/or the Investment Company has its registered seat or central administration. According to the EU Regulation on the law applicable to contractual obligations[192] and which applies in Germany[193], the contracting parties are allowed to choose the applicable national law. The choice must be made expressly or clearly demonstrated by the terms of the contract or the circumstances of the case.[194] To the extent that the law applicable to the contract has not been determined by the parties, contracts for the provision of services, such as investment management, are governed by the law of the country where the service provider has its habitual residence. This is the place of the Investment Company's central administration.

7.3.3.1.2 Legal relationship between investor and distributor or other fund service provider

Breach of contractual duty

The investor may have a claim for damages against a fund distributor or other service provider for breach of a duty arising from a distribution or other service contract.

---

[192] Regulation (EC) No 593/2008 of the European Parliament and of the Council of 17 June 2008 on the law applicable to contractual obligations (Rome I).
http://eur-lex.europa.eu/LexUriServ/LexUriServ.do?uri=OJ:L:2008:177:0006:0016:EN:PDF

[193] Article 3 para (1) no. 1. b) EGBGB in connection with §3 para (1) of Regulation (EC) no. 593/2008 of the European Parliament and of the Council of 17 June 2008 (OJ EU L 177 of 04.07.2008 p. 6) on the law applicable to contractual obligations (Rome I) and Article 27 para (1) of the EGBGB.

[194] Where all other elements relevant to the situation at the time of the choice are located in a country other than the country whose law has been chosen, the choice of the parties shall not prejudice the application of provisions of the law of that other country which cannot be derogated from by agreement. Where all other elements relevant to the situation at the time of the choice are located in one or more Member States, the parties' choice of applicable law other than that of a Member State shall not prejudice the application of provisions of Community law, where appropriate as implemented in the Member State of the forum, which cannot be derogated from by agreement. Article 3 para (3) EU Regulation on the law applicable to contractual obligations The same rule applies to consumer contracts (see chapter 9.2.1).

Applicability of German law

For foreign distributors and other service providers, the EU Regulation on the law applicable to contractual obligations[195] applies. The contracting parties are free to choose the applicable national law. In the absence of a choice of law, a distribution contract or contract for the provision of services will be governed by the law of the country where the distributor or service provider has its habitual residence. For companies and other bodies, corporate or unincorporated, this is the place of their central administration. The habitual residence of a natural person acting in the course of his business activity is his principal place of business. Where the contract is concluded through a branch or if, under the contract, performance is the responsibility of a branch, the place where the branch is located is treated as the place of habitual residence (Article 19 para (2) EU Regulation on the law applicable to contractual obligations).

Duty to disclose information or to advise the investor

The investor may have claims for damages for breach of a duty to disclose information or to advise the investor against German and foreign distributors whose contract with the investor is subject to German law (§280 para (1) BGB).

The distributor's duty to the investor to disclose information or advise may originate from an investment advisory agreement. This agreement does not have to be in any particular form and may be implied. An offer by the investor to enter into an advisory agreement can be implied if the investor approaches the distributor with the intention of discussing a possible investment, which is clearly important to the investor, and if the investor clearly relies upon the special knowledge of the distributor for its investment decision.[196] By entering into communications with the investor and advising it, the distributor may be said to have impliedly accepted this offer, especially if the distributor has a personal economic interest. It is not necessary that there is a fee arrangement.[197] An advisory agreement will not have been concluded by implication if the investor on its own initiative instructs its bank or distributor by unconditional order to buy specified units.

---

[195] Regulation (EC) No 593/2008 of the European Parliament and of the Council of 17 June 2008 on the law applicable to contractual obligations (Rome I).
http://eur-lex.europa.eu/LexUriServ/LexUriServ.do?uri=OJ:L:2008:177:0006:0016:EN:PDF
[196] Keunecke, Prospekte im Kapitalmarkt, Berlin 2005, note 529; Schödermeier/Baltzer in Brinkhaus/Scherer, see footnote 21, §20 KAGG, note 36.
[197] Schödermeier/Baltzer in Brinkhaus/Scherer, see footnote 21, §20 KAGG, note 36.

The distributor's advice has to meet the requirements of the individual investor and the particular investment.[198] It needs to take account of the personal circumstances of the investor, its knowledge and experience with other comparable transactions, its interest and readiness to assume risk. It also needs to reflect the risks of the investment which could be of material importance for a particular investor in light of its circumstances. Information and advice must be complete, accurate, rendered diligently, comprehensible and up-to-date. The distributor whose advice is based on a prospectus is obliged to check the accuracy and completeness of the prospectus.[199] Inconsistencies or mistakes in the prospectus must be expressly corrected.

Breach of pre-contractual duty

§311 para (2) in connection with §280 para (1) BGB concerns liability derived from precontractual obligations.

Applicability of German law

How these provisions apply to foreign service providers is determined by the EU Regulation on the law applicable to non-contractual obligations.[200] According to this Regulation, the law applicable to non-contractual obligations arising out of dealings prior to the conclusion of a contract is that which applies to the contract or which would have applied to it had it been entered into (Article 12 para (1) EU Regulation on the law applicable to non-contractual obligations). If the applicable law cannot be determined on this basis (Article 12 para (2) EU Regulation on the law applicable to non-contractual obligations), it shall be:

1. the law of the country in which the damage occurs, irrespective of the country in which the event giving rise to the damage occurred and irrespective of the country or countries in which the indirect consequences of that event occurred;

---

[198] Keunecke, see footnote 196, note 530; Schödermeier/Baltzer in Brinkhaus/Scherer, see footnote 21, §20 KAGG, notes 37-40.

[199] Keunecke, see footnote 196, note 531.

[200] Regulation (EC) No 864/2007 of the European Parliament and of the Council of 11 July 2007 on the law applicable to non-contractual obligations (Rome II).
http://eur-lex.europa.eu/LexUriServ/LexUriServ.do?uri=OJ:L:2007:199:0040:0049:EN:PDF

2. where the parties have their habitual residence in the same country at the time when the event giving rise to the damage occurs, the law of that country; or

3. where it is clear from all the circumstances of the case that the non-contractual obligation arising out of dealings prior to the conclusion of a contract is manifestly more closely connected with a country other than that indicated in points 1. and 2., the law of that other country.

To the extent German law applies, the following principles regarding liability for inaccurate or incomplete information are classified by the German jurisprudence as precontractual (*culpa in contrahendo*):

Breach of information duties in §121 InvG

The Investment Company and its distributors and intermediaries are responsible for the provision of information to investors before units are purchased (see chapter 6.1). The breach of these duties can result in their precontractual liability for damages.[201]

Investor's special trust in issuers and publishers of prospectuses (Prospekthaftung im engen Sinn)

Each person responsible for the distribution of a prospectus is liable for its accuracy and completeness.

The term prospectus means the full and simplified prospectus and any written (including electronic media) statements which contain material information about the investment, or which are intended to do so and which are intended to serve as basis for an investor's investment decision.[202] The investor can expect that such a document provides it with an accurate picture of the investment, that the document informs the investor accurately and completely about all the circumstances which are or could be material for its investment

---

[201] OLG Hamm, Urteil vom 31.01.2000, Az. 31 U 167/97; Schödermeier/Baltzer in Brinkhaus/Scherer, see footnote 21, §19 KAGG, note 17; Baur, see footnote 24, §19 KAGG, note 19.

[202] Hopt/Voigt, Prospekt-und Kapitalmarktinformationshaftung, Tübingen 2005, p. 197-198; Gross, see footnote 189, §47 BörsG, note 5.

decision.[203] The overall test of a reasonable average investor is determinative.[204] Marketing materials which refer to the full and simplified prospectus for further reference and which avoid the impression of providing a sufficient basis for the investor's decision should not qualify as a prospectus.[205] It is sufficient if the prospectus is circulated to a limited number of investors, for example by private placement. Its dissemination to the public is not a requirement.[206]

The respondent can be anyone responsible for the investment product or who is the issuer or publisher of a prospectus.[207] Responsibility may extend to professional experts, such as accountants, tax advisers or lawyers, who knowingly and deliberately are involved in composing the prospectus or distributing the product, and who thereby can be said to solicit the investor's special trust.[208] These persons are liable for inaccurate and incomplete statements, even if they have never met the investor and are not personally involved in the investor's purchase, because they enjoy such special trust.[209]

Investor's special trust invested in and solicited by distributors
(Prospekthaftung im weiten Sinn)

A precontractual obligation to advise and disclose can originate from special personal trust the investor places in the distributor. Such special trust may arise if the distributor gives an impression of knowledge, competence and personal reliability and/or if the distributor personally guarantees the success of the investment.[210] The behaviour has to be objectively sufficient to create a special trust which exceeds the trust normally expected during contractual negotiations.[211] In these circumstances, the distributor has a higher duty of care and is obliged to make its own inquiries and not to rely on information from third parties,

---

[203] BGH, Urteil vom 19.07.2004, Az. II ZR 218/03.
http://juris.bundesgerichtshof.de/cgi-bin/rechtsprechung/document.py?Gericht=bgh&Art=en&sid=22839ca14ad1a9ca2f300a376556b5b7&nr=29990&pos=5&anz=13
BGH, Urteil vom 19.07.2004, Az. II ZR 402/02.
http://juris.bundesgerichtshof.de/cgi-bin/rechtsprechung/document.py?Gericht=bgh&Art=en&sid=ca55ddcd263cf677686f30b99eba009a&nr=30062&pos=9&anz=13
[204] Hopt/Voigt, see footnote 202, p. 197; Schödermeier/Baltzer in Brinkhaus/Scherer, see footnote 21, §20 KAGG, note 54.
[205] Keunecke, see footnote 196, note 500; Gross, see footnote 189, §47 BörsG, note 6.
[206] Hopt/Voigt, footnote 202, p. 199.
[207] BGH, Urteil vom 31.05.1990, ZIP 1990, p. 928, 930; Keunecke, see footnote 196, note 523-526.
[208] BGH, Urteil vom 31.05.1990, ZIP 1990, p. 928, 930; Keunecke, see footnote 196, note 527; Schödermeier/Baltzer in Brinkhaus/Scherer, see footnote 21, §20 KAGG, note 51.
[209] BGH, Urteil vom 31.05.1990, ZIP 1990, p. 928, 930.
[210] BGH, Urteil vom 12.02.1986, ZIP 1986, p. 562, 563; Hopt/Voigt, see footnote 202, p. 231.
[211] Schödermeier/Baltzer in Brinkhaus/Scherer, see footnote 21, §20 KAGG, note 53.

including from prospectuses, without checking them.[212] The more trust the investor puts in the distributor, the more careful the distributor's advice must be.

Default

Under general civil law principles, defendants are liable for intent and gross negligence and for mere negligence (§§276, 278 BGB). The defendant's duty of care is, therefore, higher under civil law than under the Investment Act. Negligent ignorance of inaccurate or incomplete information can lead to liability.

Liability cannot be excluded by general terms and conditions.[213]

Burden of proof

The burden of proof generally lies on the investor claimant.

An exception is that the German High Court accepts the presumption that a prospectus which is inaccurate or incomplete in material aspects was causal in an investment decision based on it.[214] The same presumption applies to advice which has been wrongly given. It is presumed that the investor would have acted in accordance with correct advice.[215] The respondent has to prove that the damage would also have occurred if the information had been properly given, in other words that the investor would still have made the investment.

In addition, according to §280 para (1) sentence 1 BGB the burden of proof for default is shifted in that the defendant has to prove that it did not act with intent or negligence.

Scope of liability

The investor has to be put into the same position as if it had not purchased the units (*negatives Interesse*). The investor is entitled to cancel the purchase contract and reimbursement of expenses. Alternatively, the investor is entitled to keep the units and claim the difference between the unit price paid and the lower real value. The investor is also entitled to claim lost profit from alternative investments unless the defendant can

---

[212] Schödermeier/Baltzer in Brinkhaus/Scherer, see footnote 21, §20 KAGG, note 57.

[213] Outlining case law in detail: Keunecke, see footnote 196, notes 541 et seq.

[214] BGH, Urteil vom 31.05.1990, ZIP 1990, p. 928, 932.

[215] BGH, Urteil vom 17.05.1994, WM 1994, p. 1746, 1747.

prove even if its advice had been correct, the profit in question would not have been obtained.

Liability of each respondent is as a joint and several debtor.

Limitation

The limitation period for contractual claims is three years (§195 BGB). For liability arising out of an investor's special trust invested in issuers and publishers of prospectuses *(Prospekthaftung im engen Sinn),* the German High Court applies the limitation periods of §127 para (5) InvG *mutatis mutandis.*[216]

7.3.3.2 Tort

Under the EU Regulation on the law applicable to non-contractual obligations[217], the law applicable to a non-contractual obligation arising out of a tort or delict is the law of the country in which the damage occurs irrespective of the country in which the event giving rise to the damage occurred and the country or countries in which the indirect consequences of that event occur. Where it is clear from the circumstances of the case that the tort or delict is manifestly more closely connected with another country, the law of that other country applies. A manifestly closer connection with another country might be based on a pre-existing relationship between the parties such as a contract, which is closely connected with the tort or delict in question.

The basis of claim can be §823 para (2) BGB in connection with investment fraud under German criminal law or pursuant to §826 BGB, willful impairment against public order *(vorsätzliche sittenwidrige Schädigung).* However, defendants will find it difficult to establish a claim because they need to establish that the defendant acted with intent.[218]

The basis of claim can also be §823 para (2) BGB in connection with investor protective provisions *(Schutzgesetze)* contained in the Investment Act, for example the information requirements of §121 InvG (see chapter 6.1). The defendant must have breached the

---

[216] BGH, Urteil vom 18.12.2000, Az. II ZR 84/99.
http://juris.bundesgerichtshof.de/cgi-bin/rechtsprechung/document.py?Gericht=bgh&Art=en&sid=996b2bb89e9d0d21af5ef50a3a6f27fc&nr=23007&pos=2&anz=4

[217] Regulation (EC) No 864/2007 of the European Parliament and of the Council of 11 July 2007 on the law applicable to non-contractual obligations (Rome II).
http://eur-lex.europa.eu/LexUriServ/LexUriServ.do?uri=OJ:L:2007:199:0040:0049:EN:PDF

[218] Outlining case law in detail: Keunecke, see footnote 196, note 572 et seq; Hopt/Voigt, see footnote 202, p. 236; Schödermeier/Baltzer in Brinkhaus/Scherer, see footnote 21, §20 KAGG, note 67.

relevant Schutzgesetz intentionally or negligently. However, if an objective infringement of a protective provision has occurred, it is usually presumed that the defendant's conduct was blameworthy. Thus, instead of the plaintiff having to prove fault on the part of the defendant, the burden of proof is on the defendant to show that the breach was not caused by circumstances within the defendant's sphere of responsibility.[219]

The limitation period is three years.

---

[219] Palandt, see footnote 56, note 81.

CHAPTER 8 - LISTING ON A GERMAN STOCK EXCHANGE

This chapter contains a description of how Exchange Traded Funds are listed on a German stock exchange, using the example of the Frankfurt Stock Exchange (FSE), which is managed by Deutsche Börse AG.

8.1 Exchange Traded Funds

Exchange Traded Funds (ETFs) are domestic or foreign investment funds, UCITS or non-UCITS, which are tradable in exchange trading and which replicate the performance of a reference index. The underlying indices may be national or international equity, bond and real estate indices or commodity indices. Active ETFs pursue an active investment strategy, for example which aims at exceeding the performance of a reference index or replicating its performance with a variable participation rate. Most ETFs, however, pursue a passive investment strategy, whose objective is to replicate the performance of an underlying index as accurately as possible.

Passively managed ETFs aim to trade at the same price as the NAV of the underlying asset basket. The price for a single unit should correspond to a fraction of the index value defined by the issuer. Due to trading and management costs and differences in the composition of the fund and the benchmark, the performance of the ETF may differ from that of the index it replicates. Tracking error is the difference between the price performance of the ETF and the performance of the index to which it is linked. One task of the fund manager is to minimise tracking error.

Unlike traditional funds, ETFs have no front-loaded or redemption fees. A passive management strategy ensures that annual management fees for passive ETFs are lower than those for actively managed funds. The main costs are standard transaction charges for purchases or sales on the stock exchange. To minimise these, provide liquidity for the ETF and ensure that the units' market price approximates to the net asset value of the underlying assets, only large institutional investors which are authorised participants trade in ETF units on the primary market with the Investment Company, and only in "creation units", large blocks of tens of thousands of ETF units which are usually exchanged for in-kind baskets of the underlying securities. Conversely, units are redeemed by authorised participants in substantial blocks of "redemption units" against payment in-kind by the ETF of a basket of component index securities plus or minus a balancing cash element reflecting the relevant NAV. Authorised participants may invest long-term in ETF shares, but usually act as market makers for the ETF on the stock exchange, whereas other investors trade ETF units on the secondary market.

8.2 Admission to the FSE Regulated Market

8.2.1 The Regulated Market and its segments

Access to stock exchanges is gained through markets regulated by the EU (Regulated Market) or by the stock exchanges themselves (Regulated Unofficial Market, see chapter 8.9). The Regulated Market is an Organised Market in accordance with §2 para (5) WpHG. Admission and continuing obligations are regulated by law.

8.2.1.1 General Standard and Prime Standard

The Regulated Market of the FSE has two main segments, the General Standard and Prime Standard. Inclusion in the General Standard is automatic upon admission to the Regulated Market. General Standard companies predominantly target German investors. ETFs are listed on the General Standard.

The Prime Standard is tailored to the needs of companies wishing to position themselves to attract international investors. It is only open to shares and certificates representing shares. In addition to the EU requirements of the General Standard, Prime Standard issuers must comply with international standards of disclosure and transparency.

8.2.1.2 ETF & ETC Segment

ETFs are typically included in the ETF & ETC Segment of the FSE's Regulated Market. The ETF & ETC Segment is subdivided into the sub-segments "XTF Exchange Traded Funds" and "Exchange Traded Commodities". In the sub-segment XTF Exchange Traded Funds, passive ETFs und active ETFs are traded as separate product groups. A precondition for participation is that the units must be admitted to trading on the Regulated Market of the FSE.

8.2.2 Main admission requirements

ETFs which are to be traded on the Deutsche Börse's ETF segment must have been admitted to trading on the Regulated Market of the FSE. Admission is a two-stage process which consists of admission to listing and introduction to trading (see chapter 8.3).

Without approval of admission to listing, introduction to trading cannot take place. The earliest possible admission day is the stock exchange trading day following the day of receipt of the application by the Management Board.

The admission process is governed by the Stock Exchange Act (*Börsengesetz*) and the Stock Exchange Admission Regulation (*Börsenzulassungs-Verordnung*). The Act and Regulation differentiate between listings of shares in stock corporations and listings of other securities, but contain no special provisions for investment fund listings. As a result, the admission requirements for investment units slightly differ for those funds which are incorporated and issue shares and those which are not. For every individual listing the Management Board assesses the extent to which the listing rules for shares or securities may be conferred on the relevant ETF.

The most important conditions for admissions to the Regulated Market are as follows:

8.2.2.1 Free transferability and minimum number of securities

Units must be freely transferable within the meaning of Article 35 of the Regulation (EC) no. 1287/2006[220].

The minimum number of units to be admitted must be at least 10,000 (§2 para (3) Stock Exchange Admission Regulation). The Management Board may admit a lower number, if it is satisfied that there will be an adequate market for the securities. ETFs are open-end investment funds which continuously sell and redeem units. The number of units they can issue is unlimited and the number of units outstanding varies every day. Admission to listing is therefore granted for up to a certain number of units. The headroom must be sufficient to allow for the ETF to grow through the duration of its listing.

8.2.2.2 Issuer's existence for at least three years

For incorporated investment funds, the Investment Company as issuer of shares must have existed as an incorporated enterprise and must have published its financial statements for at least three financial years in accordance with applicable law. If the issuer is not incorporated in Germany, the Management Board may require a legal opinion from an independent law firm confirming that applicable foreign publication requirements have been met. International issuers can present their financial statements in accordance with

---

[220] See footnote 19.

IAS/IFRS (EC Regulation 809/2004) or accounting standards equivalent to IAS/IFRS as set out by the EU (EC Regulation 1606/2002).

The Management Board can grant exceptions if it is in the interest of the issuer and the public, for example if the Management Board is satisfied that investors have information to be able to arrive at an informed judgment on the issuer and the securities. This condition should frequently be fulfilled in relation to ETFs, since existing for three years is not so much a seal of quality for collective investment schemes as it is for business companies. Some ETFs are designed to have a limited term with enforced redemption of shares on a specified date. For investors in ETFs which typically publish a prospectus, annual and semi-annual reports, the information provided in such documents should be sufficient for investors to come to an investment decision.

8.2.2.3 Non-EU / EEA ETFs

Shares of incorporated investment funds domiciled outside the EU and EEA which are not listed on a stock exchange comparable to an Organised Market in accordance with §2 para (5) WpHG in their country of origin or in the country which represents their main market, can only be admitted to listing if they can deliver *prima facie* evidence to the Management Board that admittance in such countries was not denied for reasons of investor protection.

8.2.2.4 Listing agent

Application for admission to listing is filed jointly by the issuer and a listing agent. The listing agent must be a German credit institution, a financial services institution, or the German branch of a foreign credit or financial services institution. The listing agent must be admitted to trading on the FSE and able to provide evidence of liable equity capital of at least EUR 730,000. Issuers which are already listed on the Regulated Market at one German exchange may apply for admission to another exchange without a listing agent. Typically, the listing agent will be the ongoing institutional contact between the exchange and the issuer while the listing is maintained.

8.2.2.5 No listing prospectus

Pursuant to §32 para (3) no. 2 BörsG in connection with §1 para (2) no. 1 and para (3) Securities Prospectus Act (WpPG), no listing prospectus is required for admission of foreign investment funds within the meaning of the Investment Act to the Regulated Market of a German stock exchange.

The Management Board generally requires the prospectus for investment funds which have one available to be delivered to it for information purposes. The German full and simplified prospectus including any addenda in respect of UCITS funds which have been notified for public distribution to the BaFin should, therefore, be filed with the exchange. For non-UCITS funds which have been notified to the BaFin, the German full prospectus including any addenda should be made available to the exchange.

Foreign investment funds which have not or cannot be notified for public distribution with the BaFin (see chapter 2.1.2.2) and are considering a listing on the Regulated Market of a German stock exchange without a prospectus are subject to applicable private placement rules (see chapter 3).

8.2.3 Applications

8.2.3.1 Application to the Regulated Market

The Investment Company as issuer should complete the "Application for admission of securities to trading in the Regulated Market" and file it with the Management Board (§60 para (2) Exchange Rules for the FSE[221]). The form is available on the FSE website in German and English.[222] Information about the issuer, the listing agent, the securities and the type of admission (General or Prime Standard) must be inserted. The application should be signed by the issuer and the listing agent and accompanied by the documents listed below (§48 of the German Stock Exchange Admission Regulation).

Foreign applicants are permitted to provide information to the FSE in English. However, if the ETF has been notified to the BaFin for public distribution, the Investment Company will have those German translations at its disposal which were used for the BaFin notification. These translations should also be made available to the Management Board. If any of the following documents are not available in German or English, the applicant must prepare certified English language translations:

---

[221] Exchange Rules for the Frankfurter Wertpapierbörse (FWB), 15 December 2009
http://deutsche-boerse.com/INTERNET/EXCHANGE/zpd.nsf/KIR+Web+Publikationen+E/
HAMN-52CDY7/$FILE/FWB01e_09-12-15.pdf?OpenElement

[222] German:
http://deutsche-boerse.com/INTERNET/EXCHANGE/zpd.nsf/KIR+Web+Publikationen/
RJAN-5NFBKE/$FILE/Zulassungsantrag_01_01_2010.pdf?OpenElement
English:
http://deutsche-boerse.com/INTERNET/EXCHANGE/zpd.nsf/KIR+Web+Publikationen+E/
RJAN-5NFBKE/$FILE/Zulassungsantrag_englisch_01_01_2010.pdf?OpenElement

1. current certified extract from the Investment Company's commercial register or equivalent if a commercial register does not exist in the country of origin. The Management Board is entitled to require a legal opinion from an independent law firm confirming equivalence;

2. current company memorandum and articles of association of the Investment Company or equivalent for an international issuer if these do not exist in the company's country of origin. If the ETF is in contractual form, the memorandum and articles of the fund should be filed in addition. §1 of the Stock Exchange Admission Regulation requires that the incorporation itself and the related documents must comply with the laws of the country in which the company has its registered office. The Management Board is entitled to require a legal opinion from an independent law firm to this effect;

3. any permits or deeds of authorisation required for the incorporation of the Investment Company, for the lawful exercise of its business activities or where the issue of the securities requires governmental authorisation;

4. evidence of the legal basis for the issue of the units. The units must have been issued in accordance with applicable law (§4 of the Stock Exchange Admission Regulation). Since foreign legal systems may differ from Germany, the Management Board is entitled to require a legal opinion confirming that the units were validly issued;

5. statement if there is a global certificate for the securities to be admitted and how the securities are deposited;

6. if the ETF is in corporate form, reports on the incorporation of the issuer and their audit, if the issuer has not existed as a company for at least three years (see exemption in chapter 8.2.2.2); and

7. if the issuer and/or the listing agent is/are represented by an agent, a written power of attorney must be included in the application file.

The documents must be sent to the Management Board with the subscription form. The documents can be delivered in advance by fax or e-mail and must subsequently be delivered by mail.

The Management Board might require additional documents from the applicant. Investment funds which have a prospectus are generally required to deliver it to the Management Board for information purposes (see chapter 8.2.2.5). Investment funds which have been notified for public distribution to the BaFin should provide the stock exchange with the German full prospectus and in case of a UCITS the German simplified prospectus also, each with addenda or supplements.

The Management Board publishes the admission at the issuer's expense in the *elektronischer Bundesanzeiger*.

8.2.3.2 Application to Deutsche Börse's ETF segment

8.2.3.2.1 Investment Company and Deutsche Börse AG agreement

The Investment Company can apply for admission to the ETF segment of the Regulated Market. The listing requirements are set out in the Deutsche Börse AG's leaflet "Exchange Traded Funds & Exchange Traded Products Segment, Conditions for Participation".[223] Participation is effected by the conclusion of an agreement between the Investment Company and Deutsche Börse AG on the terms of the Conditions for Participation. The Investment Company agrees to these conditions by completing and signing the "Application for Participation in the Exchange Traded Funds & Exchange Traded Products Segment".[224]

A term sheet as set out in Appendix 1 to the Conditions for Participation should be attached to the application, containing detailed information about the ETF and its underlying index (including iNAV, taxation, fee structure, income distribution), the issuer, distribution channels (including listings on other exchanges or Organised Markets) and designated sponsors. Applicants must electronically transfer to Deutsche Börse AG the full and, in the case of UCITS the simplified prospectus, each as filed with the BaFin as part of the notification of the fund for public distribution. Deutsche Börse AG may require additional information, for instance about the form, contractual structure, composition or trading of the units.

---

[223] http://deutsche-boerse.com/INTERNET/EXCHANGE/zpd.nsf/KIR+Web+Publikationen+E/HAMN-52FAZ6/$FILE/2009-12-01_ETF_ETP_Segment_Conditions_for_Participation.pdf?OpenElement

[224] http://deutsche-boerse.com/Deutsche Börse AG/dispatch/en/binary/gdb_content_pool/imported_files/public_files/10_downloads/31_trading_member/10_Products_and_Functionalities/40_Xetra_Funds/ETF_ETP_Segment_Application_Form.pdf

8.2.3.2.2 Permission of the ETF for public distribution

Only investment funds which have been notified to the BaFin for public distribution can be included in the ETF segment of the Regulated Market. The listing application to the Regulated Market must take place in conjunction with the BaFin notification. Admission can only take effect on or after the date on which the fund units are permitted for public distribution in Germany, which for UCITS is two months after the filing of the BaFin notification and for non-UCITS three months thereafter, provided in each case that the BaFin does not prohibit public distribution of the ETF.

8.2.3.2.3 Information to be submitted on a daily basis, iNAV

Prior to the start of trading, the Investment Company is obliged to provide Deutsche Börse AG with the information set out in Appendix 2 to the Conditions for Participation on a daily basis in electronic form. This includes the ISIN and number of securities held by the ETF, the ETF's cash component, assets under management stated in EUR, and the NAV as of the last trading day.

The Investment Company is required continuously, at least once every 60 seconds, to calculate the iNAV of the ETF units and to make the data available to trading participants at the FSE. iNAVs state the current value of the fund assets and are usually calculated on the basis of the current prices of the individual items contained in the fund portfolio. iNAV must be calculated and distributed throughout the whole period that the fund units are traded. Its requirements are determined pursuant to Appendix 3 to the Conditions for Participation. Third parties may be appointed to calculate and distribute iNAV. Deutsche Börse AG, for example, offers this service under its iNAV® brand.

8.2.3.2.4 Designated sponsor

For ETFts to be traded in the electronic trading system Xetra, evidence is required that at least one designated sponsor will support the units. Designated sponsors stabilise temporary market imbalances between supply and demand and improve liquidity by quoting bid and offer prices. They also post quotes in the system, whether at the sponsor's initiative, if a market participant makes a quote request, or during auctions. This activity assists the continuous trading of the issuer's securities. As part of this process, the designated sponsor and the ETF provider exchange baskets of securities for ETF shares and vice versa.

Designated Sponsors must be admitted by the FSE for sponsoring these securities. Admission is available to all banks, broker firms and securities trading houses admitted to trading on Xetra®. The application by the designated sponsor, the sample contract for which is also available on the FSE website[225], should be filed no later than the date on which the listing application is made with the FSE. Admission and the rights and obligations of the designated sponsor are governed by §§145, 146 of the FSE's Exchange Rules.

The Investment Company has to evidence in its application for admission that it has appointed at least one designated sponsor as liquidity provider for the ETF units. To achieve this, the Investment Company and the designated sponsor sign a service contract, a sample of which is available in English on the FSE website[226]. The sample contract between the issuer and the designated sponsor provided by Deutsche Börse AG suggests additional areas where they may co-operate at their discretion. The designated sponsor may assist the issuer in complying with FSE rules and regulations, and its obligations arising from the admission to listing (see chapter 8.5), public and investor relations, reports and press releases, research, distributing the issuer's securities, and organising general meetings.

8.3 Trading

After the investment units have been admitted to the Regulated Market, they can be introduced to trading at the earliest on the stock exchange trading day following the first publication of the prospectus (§52 German Stock Exchange Admission Regulation). ETFs are traded on the electronic platform Xetra.

---

[225] http://xqs.deutsche-boerse.com/xfmws/binary/de/07_Markets_Services_-_Member_Services_+_Admission/FWB/12g_FWB_Beauftragung_als_Designated_Sponsor.pdf
http://xqs.deutsche-boerse.com/xfmws/binary/de/07_Markets_Services_-_Member_Services_+_Admission/FWB/FWB_Antrag_Designated_Sponsor_08_08.pdf
[226] http://deutsche-boerse.com/Deutsche Börse
AG/dispatch/en/binary/gdb_content_pool/imported_files/public_files/10_downloads/31_trading_member/30_Market_Making/20_Stocks/10_Designated_Sponsors/DS_Formulare/SampleContract.pdf

The Investment Company must file an "Application to introduction of admitted securities to trading on the regulated market (Listing)" [227] with the Management Board. The subscription form is available in German and English. Foreign applicants are permitted to provide information in English. The issuer must notify the Management Board when the securities to be issued will be launched and about their main features. The Management Board publishes its decision about the introduction to trading on the internet (www.deutsche-boerse.com).

The admission of securities to the stock exchange expires three months after its publication if the securities are not admitted to trading within this period. The Managing Board has the power to grant a reasonable extension of this time period if the issuer can show a justifiable reason for the extension (§38 para (4) BörsG).

8.4 Clearing and settlement

Xetra has an integrated clearing house, Eurex Clearing AG, which provides for the netting of receivables and liabilities (clearing) for transactions executed on FSE. Eurex Clearing AG acts directly as central counterparty (CCP) between the trading parties and offsets purchases and sales upon conclusion of a transaction. The transaction parties' counterparty risk is therefore limited to the CCP. The clearing system of Eurex Clearing AG, with its integrated safety and control systems, ensures that trades executed on the ETF market will close.

Delivery and cash transfer (settlement) for trades concluded on FSE occurs through the German central securities depository, Clearstream Banking AG. Admission to collective safe custody (*Girosammelverwahrung*) is a prerequisite for any ETF listing. There are three ways in which foreign ETFs can be admitted to collective safe custody:

1. the original ETF certificate is deposited with Clearstream Banking AG, Frankfurt;

2. the original ETF certificate is included in Central Securities Depository (CSD) link, so that there is a direct account connection between Clearstream

---

[227] German:
http://deutsche-boerse.com/INTERNET/EXCHANGE/zpd.nsf/KIR+Web+Publikationen/HAMN-78J9RT/$FILE/Antragsformular+Notierungsaufnahme01_01_2010.pdf?OpenElement
English:
http://deutsche-boerse.com/INTERNET/EXCHANGE/zpd.nsf/KIR+Web+Publikationen+E/HAMN-78J9RT/$FILE/Antragsformular+Notierungsaufnahme01_01_2010_englisch.pdf?OpenElement

Banking AG, Frankfurt and the foreign central depository pursuant to §5 para (4) of the German Law on the Deposit and Acquisition of Securities (*Depotgesetz*), provided that the original certificate is kept with the foreign CSD. If this not possible, then it may be necessary to prepare an additional global certificate; and

3. The ETF can be admitted to collective safe custody through issuance of German Depository Receipts (*Deutsche Zertifikate*).

The contact details of the Securities Admission Department of Clearstream Banking AG and a list of the documents and information required for the admission to collective safe custody are set out in the special leaflet dated 2 December 2002, "XTF Exchange Traded Funds – Clearing and Settlement"[228].

8.5 Ongoing obligations following the listing

8.5.1 General Standard

Companies listed in the General Standard have to comply with follow-up obligations. The most important duties as regards investors, the Exchange and the BaFin are summarised in this chapter 8.5. They are set out in the German Securities Trading Act (*Wertpapierhandelsgesetz, WpHG*) and explained by the BaFin in its Issuer Guidelines (*Emittentenleitfaden*) dated 20 May 2009.[229]

§41 BörsG sets out the issuer and listing agent's obligations to provide the Management Board with all information within their area of competence and knowledge necessary for proper performance of their duties in relation to the admission and introduction of the securities. One consequence of this rule is that information made available to the public also must be delivered to the FSE without undue delay.

The Management Board can require the issuer of admitted securities to publish information in a manner and timeframe as the Management Board considers necessary to protect the

---

[228] http://www10.deutsche-boerse.com/INTERNET/EXCHANGE/zpd.nsf/Web+Publikationen/SKRS-5HEJDU/$FILE/XTF_Clearing_and_Settlement.pdf?OpenElement

[229] Issuer Guidelines
http://www.bafin.de/cln_152/SharedDocs/Downloads/DE/Service/Leitfaeden/emittentenleitfaden__2009,templateId=raw,property=publicationFile.pdf/emittentenleitfaden_2009.pdf

public or for proper stock exchange dealing. If the issuer does not comply, after hearing the issuer the Management Board can make the publication itself at the issuer's expense.

8.5.1.1 Publication of annual report

8.5.1.1.1 Addressees

§37v WpHG applies to foreign Investment Companies whose units are only listed on an Organised Market in Germany and not in any other EU or EEA Member State, and to foreign Investment Companies which are also listed in another EU/EEA Member State, but have chosen Germany as their home country pursuant to §2b WpHG.

8.5.1.1.2 Contents

The Investment Company as issuer must publish its audited annual financial report within four months of the end of its financial year on an internet website, which the BaFin recommends is that of the Investment Company. The annual financial report must contain at least:

1. the annual financial statements prepared and audited in accordance with the national law of the state in which the company has its registered seat;

2. the management report; and

3. a compliance statement by the legal representatives of the issuer that the annual report reflects the true state of the company's affairs made in accordance with the provisions of §264 para (2) sentence 3, §289 para (1) sentence 5 HGB.

The compliance statement can be written by adapting the model of the near final draft German Accounting Standard (*Deutscher Rechnungslegungsstandard – DRS*) no. 16, paragraph 56, on consolidated financial statements[230][231].

To the extent a parent company is obliged to publish consolidated financial statements under the national law of the state in which it has its registered seat, the rules of §37v are modified by §37y WpHG. The annual financial report must also contain the audited consolidated financial statements prepared in accordance with Regulation (EC) no. 1606/2002[232], i.e. IAS and IFRS, the group management report and a compliance statement made in accordance with the provisions set out in §297 para (2) sentence 3, §315 para (1) sentence 6 HGB.

If the annual report or the consolidated financial statements are issued by a non-EU/EEA issuer and audited by a non EU/EEA auditor, the report has to include a confirmation by the German auditors' chamber (*Wirtschaftsprüferkammer*) pursuant to §134 para (2a) German Auditors' Regulation (*Wirtschaftsprüferordnung*, WPO) on the registry entry of the relevant auditor in the German auditors' register or on his dispensation from such entry pursuant to §134 para (4) sentence 8 WPO.

The BaFin has the power to exempt an issuer with its registered seat in a non-EU/EEA country from the requirements regarding the contents of the annual report and the consolidated financial statements, provided that it is subject to equivalent rules or if it submits to such rules in that country. The information to be prepared pursuant to the provisions of that third country must still be made available to the German public, the BaFin and the company register in the same manner and subject to the same requirements as to notice and timing as described in this chapter 8.5.1.1.

---

[230] *Bekanntmachung des Deutschen Rechnungslegungsstandards Nr. 16 (DRS 16) – Zwischenberichterstattung – des Deutschen Rechnungslegungs Standards Committees e.V., Berlin, nach §342 Abs. 2 des HGB vom 08.07.2008; veröffentlicht als Beilage zum Bundesanzeiger vom 24.07.2008.* http://www.standardsetter.de/drsc/docs/press_releases/DRS16_nearfinaldraft_180707_mitAnpassung.pdf

[231] See Issuer Guidelines XIV.3.1.3 (footnote 38) and BaFin Frequently Asked Questions of 22.01.2008 on secs. 37v et seq of the Securities Trading Act following the entry into force of the Transparency Directive Implementation Act on 20 January 2007: Häufige Fragen zur Finanzberichterstattung, issued 15.02.2008. http://www.bafin.de/cln_152/nn_722564/SharedDocs/Downloads/DE/Unternehmen/BoersennotierteUnternehmen/Finanzberichterstattung/faq_finanzberichterstattung,templateId=raw,property=publicationFile.pdf/faq_finanzberichterstattung.pdf

[232] Regulation (EC) no. 1606/2002 of the European Parliament and of the Council of 19 July 2002 on the application of international accounting standards. http://eur-lex.europa.eu/LexUriServ/LexUriServ.do?uri=OJ:L:2002:243:0001:0004:en:PDF

Neither the Securities Trading Act nor the Securities Trading Reporting and Insider List Ordinance refer to the language of the annual report and consolidated financial statements. Consequently, these documents can be published in their original language version.

8.5.1.1.3 Announcements

Prior to making the annual report or the consolidated financial statements publicly available for the first time, the Investment Company must make an EU and EEA-wide publication of when and the website where the documents will be publicly available (for details as to the mode and language of the publication see §3a, §3b and §22 *Wertpapierhandelsanzeige- und Insiderverzeichnisverordnung* – WpAIV, Securities Trading Reporting and Insider List Ordinance). Issuers which have their registered seat outside Germany are permitted to make the publication in English. The BaFin considers that notice of at least one week by an issuer to the public that its annual financial report will be available on the internet is reasonable.

The German legislator has not regulated the manner or frequency of publication. The BaFin suggests that Europe-wide dissemination of information will normally be made through a "media package": electronically, through a direct news provider or a news agency, in print and/or through a financial website. The BaFin recommends that dissemination of information should as a minimum comprise all of the above and at least one provider per means of publication. Of these, at least one must enable dissemination of the information across the EU and EEA. The issuer can use an information service provider to manage the supply of information on its behalf. The issuer's circumstances, for example its shareholding structure or how many listings it has and where, may mean that the issuer has to use additional means of communication.

The announcement must state exactly how the public can access the annual report or consolidated financial statements. A reference to a website which requires another search to access the document is not sufficient, unless the initial website leads to a page on which only the relevant financial reports are to be found and if the investor can identify the relevant report with no further search or validation by one further click. A link to the company's investor relations page which will then require another search will not satisfy the requirements.

8.5.1.1.4 Notification of the BaFin, stock exchange and company register

Simultaneously with the above announcement, the issuer must notify the BaFin (for details of the BaFin notice see §3c and §23 *Wertpapierhandelsanzeige- und Insiderverzeichnisverordnung* – WpAIV, Securities Trading Reporting and Insider List Ordinance) and the stock exchange. The notification has to be made in German (§23 para (1) VwVfG), although in practice the stock exchanges will generally accept notifications in English.

The issuer must transmit the announcement without undue delay but not before its publication, to the company register within the meaning of §8b HGB. The issuer must also transmit the annual report to the company register without undue delay, but again not before its publication.

8.5.1.1.5 Infringements

The sanction for willful and grossly negligent breaches of the above publication and notification rules is an administrative fine of up to EUR200,000 (§39 para (2) and (4) WpHG).

8.5.1.2 Information necessary for exercising rights attached to listed securities

8.5.1.2.1 Addressees

The WpHG rules outlined in this chapter 8.5.1.2 apply to foreign Investment Companies whose units are only listed on an Organised Market in Germany and not in any other EU or EEA Member State, and to foreign Investment Companies which are also listed in another EU/EEA Member State, but have chosen Germany as their home country pursuant to §2b WpHG.

Irrespective of the above, the rules outlined in chapters 8.5.1.2.2 and 8.5.1.2.3 pursuant to §30d WpHG also apply to issuers whose registered seat is in another EU/EEA Member State and whose units are listed on an Organised Market in Germany, to the extent the Home Member State does not apply equivalent information requirements.

8.5.1.2.2 Issuer's obligations to security holders

Pursuant to §30a para (1) WpHG, the Investment Company must ensure that:

1. all holders of admitted securities are treated equally under equal circumstances;

2. facilities and information to enable the holders of admitted securities to exercise their rights are publicly available in Germany;

3. data on the holders of admitted securities are protected from access by unauthorised persons; and

4. so long as securities are admitted to listing, at least one German credit or financial services institution or German branch of a non-German credit or financial services institution is appointed as paying agent in Germany, with authority to effect all necessary measures as paying agent in respect of securities, free of charge to holders of the securities.

   In practical terms, the paying agent can be the same institution that is appointed as paying and, if applicable, information agent, for the fund's registration for public distribution with the BaFin (see chapter 4.2). The agent's role in relation to the listing is, however, largely notional, because ETF units are not materialised and payments to authorised participants are mainly in kind. For foreign issuers, the paying agent may also be appointed as agent for service of process in Germany.

The BaFin can exempt issuers domiciled in a non-EU/EEA country from the duties set forth in §30a WpHG if such issuers are subject to equivalent rules of that country or submit to such rules (§30f para (1) WpHG).

The sanction for willful and grossly negligent breaches of the issuer's duties in nos. 2., 3. and 4. above is an administrative fine of up to EUR100,000 (§39 para (2) and (4) WpHG).

8.5.1.2.3 Amendments to the issuer's constitutive documents

§30c WpHG requires the Investment Company to notify the BaFin and the admission offices of the domestic and foreign Organised Markets on which its units are admitted to trading, of any intended amendments to its articles of association or other constitutive documents which would affect unitholder rights. The issuer must make these notifications without undue delay following the decision to present such amendments to the constitutive or other body which will determine whether to approve them, and at the latest when such body meets to consider the amendments. The notification has to be made in German (§23 para (1) VwVfG), although in practice the stock exchange admission offices generally accept notifications in English. The FSE interprets the phrase "changes that would affect unitholder rights" broadly.

The sanction for willful and grossly negligent breaches of the issuer's notification duties is an administrative fine of up to EUR50,000 (§39 para (2) and (4) WpHG).

8.5.1.2.4 Publication of additional information

§30e WpHG requires the Investment Company to give notice without undue delay of the following matters through publication which will disseminate the information within the EU and EEA:

1. any change in the rights attached to the admitted securities or to the terms of the securities, in particular changes to the interest rates or associated conditions, provided that the rights attached to such securities are indirectly affected;

2. issue or guarantee of new or additional borrowing, except for government bonds within the meaning of §36 BörsG; and

3. information which the issuer only makes public in a third country which may be of importance to the public in the EU and the EEA.

Issuers which have their registered seat outside Germany can make the publication in English (for details about the manner and language of the publication see §3a, §3b and §26 *Wertpapierhandelsanzeige- und Insiderverzeichnisverordnung* – WpAIV, Securities Trading Reporting and Insider List Ordinance).

Simultaneously with the publication, the issuer must inform the BaFin about the relevant circumstances (for details about the BaFin notice see §3c and §26 *Wertpapierhandel-sanzeige- und Insiderverzeichnisverordnung* – WpAIV, Securities Trading Reporting and Insider List Ordinance). The BaFin notification must be in German (§23 para (1) VwVfG).

In addition, the issuer must transmit such information without undue delay but not before it has been made public, to the company register within the meaning of §8b HGB.

The BaFin can exempt issuers domiciled in a non-EU/EEA country from the duties set out in 1. and 2. above if such issuers are subject to equivalent rules in that country or submit to such rules. If exempted non-EU/EEA issuers publish information pursuant to equivalent rules, such information must be made available to the German public, the BaFin and the company register in the way described above.

The sanction for willful and grossly negligent breaches of the issuer's duty to make a BaFin notification is an administrative fine of up to EUR50,000. The sanction for breach of the issuer's publication duties and to send information to the company register is an administrative fine of up to EUR200,000 (§39 para (2) and (4) WpHG).

8.5.1.3 Insider trading, market abuse and ad hoc disclosure

Insider trading (§14 WpHG) and market abuse (§20a WpHG) are prohibited. Insider trading is punishable by imprisonment for up to five years or a criminal fine (§38 WpHG) and/or an administrative fine of up to EUR200,000. The sanction for market abuse is an administrative fine of up to EUR1,000,000 (§39 para (1), (2) and (4) WpHG).

Ad hoc disclosure pursuant to §15 WpHG is a central feature of the German Securities Trading Act. The purpose of ad hoc disclosure is to ensure all market participants have the same level of information so that they are treated equally, maintaining transparency and promoting the proper functioning of the capital markets. The sanction for willful or grossly negligent breaches of an ad hoc disclosure duty is an administrative fine of up to EUR1,000,000, and in respect of the related notification and transmission of information duties to the BaFin, the stock exchanges and the company register the sanction is an administrative fine of up to EUR200,000 (§39 para (2) an (4) WpHG). §37b and 37c WpHG contain liability clauses for damages due to failure to publish inside information without undue delay and for damages based on the publication of false inside information.

8.5.1.3.1 Ad hoc disclosure scope of application

The ad hoc disclosure requirements apply to foreign Investment Companies, provided that their units are only listed on an Organised Market in Germany and not in any other EU or EEA Member State. These requirements also apply to foreign Investment Companies which are also listed on an Organised Market in another EU/EEA Member State, provided that they have chosen Germany as their home country pursuant to §2b WpHG.

The ad hoc disclosure requirements apply to insider securities, including investment fund units admitted to trading on a German stock exchange or included in the Regulated Market (see chapter 8.8) or the Regulated Unofficial Market (see chapter 8.9). For the purposes of ad hoc disclosure, securities are deemed admitted to trading on an Organised Market or included on the Regulated Market or the Regulated Unofficial Market if the application for such admission or inclusion has been made or publicly announced.

8.5.1.3.2 Ad hoc disclosure of inside information

§15 (1) WpHG requires the issuer to publish without undue delay all inside information which directly concerns the issuer. Inside information directly concerns an issuer if it relates to developments in the issuer's operating activities. Insider information which only indirectly concerns the issuer does not have to be published, but it is still included in the insider trading prohibition (§14 WpHG). The requirements in form and content for ad hoc publication are set out in detail in the Securities Trading Reporting and Insider List Ordinance and in the Issuer Guidelines. §3b para (1) Securities Trading Reporting and Insider List Ordinance permits issuers with registered seat abroad to publish in English.

Inside information means any specific information about circumstances, current or reasonably expected to come into existence in the future, which is not public knowledge, relating to one or more issuers of insider securities, or to the insider securities themselves which, if it became publicly known, would be likely to have a significant effect on the stock exchange or market price of the relevant security. Such likelihood will be deemed to exist if a reasonable investor would take the information into account in making an investment decision.

Inside information which relates to developments outside the issuer's operating activities can still directly affect an issuer. For example, ETFs could be directly affected by developments relating to the underlying securities in the reference index. However, ETFs do not regularly receive such price sensitive information before it becomes public. The BaFin's Issuer Guidelines provide that for derivatives which are directly or indirectly based on securities of different issuers; the issuer of the derivatives has no publication obligation in relation to the underlying securities. This should equally apply to ETFs, in that there should be no publication requirement in relation to the index components. Accordingly, the publication duties for ETFs will often be limited to important information about fund structure.

An issuer or person acting on behalf or for the account of an issuer, who as part of its functions communicates or grants access to inside information to a third party, must at the same time publish the information unless the third party is contractually or by law subject to a duty to observe confidentiality. If inside information is communicated or access is granted unintentionally, the information must be published without undue delay (see IV.5.2.2 Issuer Guidelines).

8.5.1.3.3 Notification of the BaFin and stock exchanges

Before ad hoc disclosure is published, the issuer must notify the BaFin and the management of the Organised Market(s) in Germany on which the units are trading, or on which derivatives which are based on the units are trading (*Vorabmitteilung* pursuant to §15 para (4) WpHG, see 4 IV. 5 Issuer Guidelines and §8 Securities Trading Reporting and Insider List Ordinance). With the permission of the BaFin, non-German issuers may effect these notifications at the same time as the ad hoc publication, provided that this does not prejudice the decision of the Organised Market(s) concerned as regards suspension or discontinuance of stock exchange price calculation. Issuers which have not obtained such permission must also inform the management of the Organised Market(s) and the BaFin about the ad hoc disclosure at the time of the publication (§15 para (5) sentence 2 WpHG as explained in §5a Securities Trading Reporting Insider List Ordinance and and IV.6.5. Issuer Guidelines).

8.5.1.3.4 Transmission of information to the company register

The issuer must transmit inside information without undue delay but not before it is published, to the company register within the meaning of §8b HGB (§15 para (1) sentence 1 WpHG as explained in IV.6.4. Issuer Guidelines).

8.5.1.3.5 Maintenance of insider list

Pursuant to §15b WpHG, the issuer is required to maintain lists of persons working for it whose employment allows access to inside information. The issuer is obliged to update these lists without undue delay and submit them to the BaFin upon request. The issuer must inform the persons on the list about their legal obligations deriving from their access to inside information, and the legal consequences of breaches.

8.5.2 ETF segment

In addition to the continuing obligations outlined in chapter 8.2.3.2.2 of providing Deutsche Börse AG on a daily basis with certain portfolio data such as the iNAV, the Investment Company under the Conditions for Participation in the ETF segment is also required to give electronic notification without delay of any changes to the documents and information which have been submitted. Deutsche Börse AG may request additional information as to the form, contractual structure, composition or other features of the units as well as about their trading.

8.6 Revocation of admission

8.6.1 Upon application by the Investment Company (delisting)

8.6.1.1 Regulated Market (General Standard)

Upon application by an issuer, the Management Board can revoke the admission of securities to the Regulated Market (General Standard) unless investor protection concerns conflict with such revocation (§39 para (2) BörsG). The Exchange Rules of the FSE provide that there will not be investor protection concerns regarding information and notification duties, price formation and price control if after the revocation has become effective, admission of and trading in the securities will take place on another Organised Market or on a market in a non-EU country which is comparable to an Organised Market.

The FSE's Management Board will immediately publish any such revocation on its website (www.deutscheboerse.com).

The revocation of admission will take effect immediately if the affected security has been admitted to and traded on at least one other German exchange when the revocation is published. If the security has been admitted to and is being traded exclusively on a foreign Organised Market or on a comparable market in a non-EU country, the revocation will take effect three months after notice of the revocation has been published. This can be reduced to a minimum of one month as described below.

If the requirements for revocation described above are not fulfilled, investor protection will still be regarded as having been satisfied if after the decision to revoke has been announced by the issuer, investors have sufficient time to sell their securities on the Regulated Market of FSE. In such circumstances, revocation becomes effective six months after notice of the revocation has been published. This can be reduced to a minimum of three months as described below.

Upon application from the issuer, the FSE's Management Board may shorten the periods specified above if the issuer or major shareholder makes a purchase offer to the security holder, the terms of which can be reviewed in separate proceedings, for example arbitration, or if the terms of the security provide for the issuer to repurchase the security for sufficient cash compensation.

The issuer is responsible for providing evidence that the conditions for revoking the admission have been satisfied and for calculating the relevant periods. The Management Board of the FSE may require declarations and documents to be submitted by the issuer.

8.6.1.2 ETF segment

Participation in the ETF segment can be terminated by the issuer at any time with three months notice. Its right to terminate with good cause is not affected. Irrespective of which party triggered the termination, fees which have already been paid to the stock exchange are not required to be refunded. Any termination must be made in writing.

8.6.2 Revocation of admission ex officio by the Management Board

8.6.2.1 Regulated Market (General Standard)

The Management Board of the FSE has the power to revoke the lawful admission of securities to the Regulated Market (General Standard) if orderly long-term exchange trading is no longer guaranteed and the FSE's Management Board has halted trading on the Regulated Market or the issuer does not meet its obligations following the listing (see chapter 8.5), even after an appropriate time period has passed (§39 para (1) BörsG). The Management Board will publish any such revocation on its website immediately (www.deutscheboerse.com).

8.6.2.2 ETF segment

Deutsche Börse AG is entitled to require that the participation of securities in the ETF segment is terminated upon good cause, including if:

1. conditions for participation in the ETF segment do not exist or have ceased to exist retroactively at the time the agreement was concluded; or

2. it would be contrary to the interests and purposes of the ETF segment if the agreement were to continue or further securities were to be included in the ETF segment.

Termination of securities participating in the ETF segment does not affect the admission of such securities to the Regulated Market.

8.7 Fees

The Investment Company must pay an admission fee of EUR 3,000 for the admission, and an introduction fee of EUR 500 for the trading of its units pursuant to §§11 and 14 of the Fee Regulations for the FSE.[233]

A revocation fee of EUR 3,000 is payable to the FSE pursuant to §13 of the Fee Regulations for the FSE when the admission of units to the Regulated Market or a segement of the Regulated Market is revoked at the issuer's request. The *ex officio* revocation fee payable to the FSE in respect of the Regulated Market or one of its segments is EUR 2,500.

8.8 Inclusion of ETFs into the Regulated Market

Under §33 BörsG and §73 et seq Exchange Rules for the FSE, securities which are not admitted to FSE's Regulated Market may be included in trading on the Regulated Market upon application by a registered trading participant or *ex officio* by the Management Board. Securities may be included if they are admitted:

1. to trading on a Regulated Market on another German stock exchange;

2. to trading on an Organised Market in another EU or EEA Member State; or

3. to a market in another non-EU country, provided that prerequisites for admission and notification and transparency obligations comparable to those existing in the Regulated Market for admitted securities exist in such market, and the exchange of information with the competent authorities of the respective country for the purpose of monitoring trading is ensured; and

4. no circumstances are known which, should the securities be admitted, would lead to a fraud on the public or damage to substantial public interests.

---

[233] http://deutsche-boerse.com/INTERNET/EXCHANGE/zpd.nsf/KIR+Web+Publikationen+E/ HAMN-5NLGBC/$FILE/FWB12e-10-01-01.pdf?OpenElement

The FSE's Management Board decides on the inclusion of the securities and notifies the issuer of the securities accordingly. The issuer has no right to object to the decision of the Management Board. The Management Board of the FSE will publish on its website (www.deutscheboerse.com) that the securities have been included.

If a trading participant applies for inclusion of securities to trading on the Regulated Market, it has to indicate if provisions exist about reporting directors' dealings in other jurisdictions in which the securities are listed comparable to those of §15 a WpHG (see chapter 8.5.1.3), and how such dealings must be published. Any changes to the form or method of publication must be notified immediately to the FSE's Management Board.

The applicant is also required to notify the FSE's Management Board immediately of any circumstances disclosed by the issuer of the included securities or of which the applicant has otherwise become aware which are material in evaluating the included securities. This includes notifications and changes pursuant to §§30b, 30c WpHG (see chapter 8.5.1.2.3), publications and notifications pursuant to §15 WpHG (see chapter 8.5.1.3) and comparable provisions for the protection of the public and to ensure orderly exchange trading which apply in the foreign market to which the included securities are already admitted.

The applicant must also notify the trading participants immediately in an easily accessible and appropriate manner of all circumstances notified by it to the Management Board.

Since the securities are included in the Regulated Market without the issuer's consent, it does not have to comply with any continuing listing obligations. However, once the fund units are included in the Regulated Market, they are considered insider securities under the German Securities Trading Act. Consequently, the reporting requirement rules apply for own account securities transactions (§9 WpHG), insider dealing (§§12, 14, 16 and 16b WpHG), market manipulation (§20a WpHG) and analysis of financial instruments (§34b WpHG). These provisions are of general application and apply to the issuer, brokers and market makers.

The Management Board will revoke the inclusion of the securities if the applicant for inclusion in the Regulated Market applies for such revocation. The Management Board can revoke the inclusion *ex officio* if orderly long-term exchange trading is no longer guaranteed and the Management Board has halted trading on the Regulated Market. Another ground for revocation is if the trading participant does not meet its continuing obligations for the inclusion, after an appropriate grace period has expired. The revocation will be published immediately by the Management Board on its website (www.deutsche-boerse.com).

8.9 Inclusion of ETFs into the Regulated Unofficial Market

ETFs may be listed on the Regulated Unofficial Market (Open Market or *Freiverkehr*), a second German market segment regulated by law. A German stock exchange may choose to provide for this type of segment in accordance with §48 BörsG, if the securities to be included are neither listed nor included in the Regulated Market and as long as orderly trading and business conduct can be guaranteed. The BaFin monitors shares traded on the Open Market for compliance with the rules on insider trading and market abuse. Price calculation is monitored by the Market Surveillance Office (*HüSt*).

Private law governs the inclusion of securities in the Open Market. For the FSE the applicable provisions are the General Terms and Conditions of Deutsche Börse AG for the Regulated Unofficial Market on the Frankfurter Wertpapierbörse of 12 October 2009 (General Terms and Conditions of the Regulated Unofficial Market).[234] The Regulated Unofficial Market of the FSE has two trading segments, the First Quotation Board and the Entry Standard. The Entry Standard is available only for shares and certificates representing shares. Admission and continuing obligations are more onerous in the Entry Standard. The price of fund units is determined on the electronic trading system by continuous auction.

Application for inclusion of securities in the Open Market is made by a registered trading member of the FSE. The inclusion of units in investment funds can only be made by specialists commissioned by the FSE. The consent of the issuer is not necessary for inclusion in the First Quotation Board. Securities may be included in the Open Market without the issuer's knowledge. If the issuer on notice objects to the inclusion, its objection is not binding on the stock exchange. The applicant needs to prove the issuer's consent by its written approval for admission to the Entry Standard. The issuer has to contract in writing with a recognised Deutsche Börse listing partner complying with the minimum contents set out in Annex 3 of the General Terms and Conditions of the Regulated Unofficial Market.

Only securities which are not admitted or included in the Regulated Market of FSE can be included in the Open Market. Fund units may be included if they are allowed to be publicly distributed in Germany, and provided that the securities satisfy the following conditions:

---

[234] http://deutsche-boerse.com/INTERNET/EXCHANGE/zpd.nsf/KIR+Web+Publikationen+E/
HAMN-52FAGV/$FILE/FWBe10_09-10-12.pdf?OpenElement

1. an International Securities Identification Number (ISIN) has been allocated;

2. they are unofficially tradable;

3. the orderly completion of the transactions is guaranteed;

4. there are no regulatory prohibitions against trading on the Exchange; and

5. the fund units are already admitted for trading to or included in a German or foreign exchange market on which securities may be purchased or sold, or if there is a prospectus which is approved by a German or foreign authority recognised by Deutsche Börse AG. The prospectus must have been published no more than 12 months previously in German or English, or contain a summary in German or English. In the absence of such a prospectus, the applicant must prepare summary information which contains details about the security and the issuer - the issuer data form. Deutsche Börse AG will set conditions as to the contents and the issuer data form, unless the issuer's securities are already included in the Open Market.

The issuer's consent is not required for inclusion of securities on the First Quotation Board, and therefore the issuer is not subject to any continuing obligations or transparency requirements (§48 para (1) sentence 2 BörsG). The issuer is, however, subject to generally applicable regulatory rules, in particular relating to insider trading and market abuse (see chapter 8.5.1.3). These responsibilities on the issuer are the reason that the issuer's right to object to the inclusion should be allowed.[235]

The applicant must inform Deutsche Börse AG about all matters relevant for an assessment of the included security or issuer such as corporate actions, including dividend payments, insolvency and changes to the executive board or supervisory board of the issuer. In the Entry Standard, the applicant also has publication duties, which require the co-operation of the issuer.

The applicant and Deutsche Börse AG can terminate the inclusion of securities in the Open Market at any time subject to an adequate notice. When assessing what notice is sufficient, factors to be considered will include the proper interests of the participant, the lead broker and the public. The right of the parties to terminate the inclusion of securities in the Open Market without notice for legitimate reason remains unaffected. Deutsche Börse AG is

---

[235] Gross, see footnote 189, §48 BörsG, note 5, who bases such right on §1004 BGB.

entitled to terminate the inclusion without notice if the conditions for inclusion have ceased to exist, orderly trading or settlement is jeopardised or the public may be seriously prejudiced. Actions for suspension of trading remain unaffected.

Thomas Söbbing

IT/IP-Rechte im Unternehmenskauf

Leitfaden für Information Technology & Software

Transfer bei Merger & Acquisitions

Diplomica 2010 / 248 Seiten / 49,50 Euro

ISBN 978-3-8366-8551-1

EAN 9783836685511

Eine Vielzahl von Unternehmenskaufverträgen (SPA/APA) behandelt das Thema der Information Technology nur am Rande und vor allem sehr rudimentär. Inhaltlich wird häufig im Abschnitt zur Information Technology lediglich eine Garantie abgegeben, dass die Information Technology des Zielunternehmens zum Zeitpunkt des Signings in der Lage ist, die betriebswirtschaftlichen Prozesse des Zielunternehmens zu betreiben und dass dafür ausreichend Softwarelizenzen vorhanden sind. Dabei ist jedem IT-Fachmann bewusst, dass der eigentliche Wert einer IT-Infrastruktur nicht nur aus den aufgezählten Assets besteht, sondern daraus, dass die IT in der Lage ist, alle Service Needs des Zielunternehmens an die Information Technology zu befriedigen und dies auch zukünftig mit angemessenen Kosten sicherzustellen.

Zielsetzung des Werkes ist es, die rechtssichere Transferierung der Information Technology inklusive Software bei Merger & Acquisitions zu gewährleisten, den M & A Prozess aus der Sicht des IT-Rechts zu begleiten und die entsprechenden Passagen in Unternehmenskaufverträgen eindeutig zu gestalten.

Wanja Daniel Dröse

Mitarbeiterkapitalbeteiligung

Formen, Ziele und rechtliche

Rahmenbedingungen

Diplomica 2010 / 96 Seiten / 49,50 Euro

ISBN 978-3-8366-7930-5

EAN 9783836679305

Die Schere zwischen Unternehmens- und Arbeitseinkommen geht seit Jahren immer weiter auseinander. Das Gesetz zur steuerlichen Förderung der Mitarbeiterkapitalbeteiligung soll dies ändern, indem Unternehmen ein Anreiz geboten wird, die Mitarbeiter stärker als bisher am Produktivvermögen zu beteiligen.

Wanja Daniel Dröse vergleicht - unter Berücksichtigung der Änderungen des im April 2009 in Kraft getretenen Gesetzes - in der vorliegenden Studie bekannte Modelle der direkten betrieblichen Mitarbeiterkapitalbeteiligungen und filtert unter festgelegten Kriterien das geeignete Modell heraus. Der neu in dem InvG verankerte Fonds für die Kapitalbeteiligung der Mitarbeiter wird hierbei von ihm mit in die Untersuchung einbezogen. Ein herausstechendes Kriterium für das gesuchte Kapitalbeteiligungsmodell ist, dass gerade tariflich Angestellte mit einer geringen Risikoneigung angesprochen werden sollen. Ergänzend widmet sich der Autor eingehend den steuerlichbetriebsverfassungsrechtlichen, tarifrechtlichen sowie darüber hinaus personalwirtschaftlichen und betriebswirtschaftlichen Aspekten.

Zielgruppe dieses Buches sind Unternehmen sowie Betriebsräte und Gewerkschaften.

jus novum **Band 8**

Tatjana Buchmüller

**Das Maßgeblichkeitsprinzip
vor dem Hintergrund
des Bilanzrechts-
modernisierungsgesetzes
(BilMoG)**

Tatjana Buchmüller

**Das Maßgeblichkeitsprinzip vor dem
Hintergrund des Bilanzrechts-
modernisierungsgesetzes (BilMoG)**

Diplomica 2010 / 104 Seiten / 49,50 Euro

ISBN 978-3-8366-8421-7

EAN 9783836684217

Am 21. Mai 2008 veröffentlichte das Bundesministerium der Justiz, nach dem am 8. November 2007 verkündigten Referentenentwurf, den lang erwarteten Regierungsentwurf eines Gesetzes zur Modernisierung des Bilanzrechts und brachte hiermit die umfangreichste Änderung des Handelsgesetzbuches seit dem Bilanzrichtlinienumsetzungsgesetz von 1985 auf den Weg.

Das neue Handelsrecht gilt als eine Alternative zu den internationalen Rechnungslegungsstandards, ohne jedoch deren Nachteile – Komplexität, Zeitaufwand, Kosten – zu übernehmen und würde somit zu einem gleichwertigen, aber praxistauglicheren und kostengünstigeren Informationsinstrument.

Tatjana Buchmüller erläutert die wichtigen Änderungen der handelsrechtlichen Vorschriften nach dem Bilanzrechtsmodernisierungsgesetz und analysiert die relevanten Auswirkungen auf die Ertragsteuern, die schon jetzt identifiziert und berücksichtigt werden können.

jus novum Band 9

Sandra Streuling

Arbeitsrechtliche Aspekte von Zielvereinbarungen

Gestaltungsmöglichkeiten des Arbeitsvertrages
und Restriktionen der Tarifbindung

Sandra Streuling

Arbeitsrechtliche Aspekte von

Zielvereinbarungen

Gestaltungsmöglichkeiten des Arbeitsvertrages

und Restriktionen der Tarifbindung

Diplomica 2010 / 100 Seiten / 49,50 Euro

ISBN 978-3-8366-8747-8

EAN 9783836687478

Gerade im Zuge der fortschreitenden Globalisierung müssen Unternehmen ihre Wettbewerbsfähigkeit sichern und sich neuen Marktanforderungen rasch anpassen. Mit Hilfe von Zielvereinbarungen können die Personalkosten in höherem Maße an der wirtschaftlichen Lage des Unternehmens ausgerichtet werden. Durch die Individualisierung des Entgelts wird gleichzeitig aber auch eine höhere Entgeltgerechtigkeit hergestellt.

Sandra Streuling schafft mit diesem Buch einen Überblick darüber, wie Zielvereinbarungskonzepte in der Praxis eingeführt und aus rechtlicher Sicht ordnungsgemäß durchgeführt werden können. Sie zeigt die rechtliche Struktur von Zielvereinbarungen, die rechtlichen Grenzen und die sich daraus für Arbeitgeber und Arbeitnehmer ergebenden Rechte und Pflichten. Das Hauptaugenmerk liegt dabei auf der Vertragsgestaltung, wobei hier die AGB-Kontrolle sowie typische Regelungsinhalte der Rahmenvereinbarung und der konkreten jährlichen Zielvereinbarung erläutert werden.

Björn Buchgeister

Werbung mit Geschäftsbeziehungen aus wettbewerbsrechtlicher Sicht

Diplomica 2010 / 108 Seiten / 39,50 Euro

ISBN 978-3-8366-8964-9

EAN 9783836689649

Unternehmen werben gerne mit ihren attraktiven Geschäftsbeziehungen. Dabei offenbaren sie ihren potentiellen Kunden, woher ihre Produkte stammen, von welchen Zulieferern Bestandteile verarbeitet worden sind oder welche Firmen die entsprechenden Waren oder Dienstleistungen verwenden bzw. in Anspruch nehmen.

Aus dieser Art der Werbung ergeben sich sowohl Chancen als auch Risiken für das werbende Unternehmen. Björn Buchgeister greift dieses spannende Thema auf, das bisher in der Literatur, trotz seiner erheblichen Relevanz für die Unternehmen, noch wenig Beachtung fand und betrachtet es sowohl unter juristischen als auch betriebswirtschaftlichen Aspekten.

Die Werbung mit Geschäftsbeziehungen wird umfassend aus markenrechtlicher und lauterkeitsrechtlicher Sicht behandelt. Hierbei werden auch mögliche Überlegungen des (rechtswidrig) Werbenden sowie des Rechteinhabers verdeutlicht.

Das Buch schließt mit praktisch verwertbaren Ergebnissen in Thesenform ab. Es richtet sich an Entscheidungsträger in der Wirtschaft, im Betrieb und an Rechtsberater.